D1207652

MODERN ACTING: A MANUAL

MODERN ACTING:
A MANUAL

BY

SOPHIE ROSENSTEIN
Division of Drama, University of Washington

LARRAE A. HAYDON
Portland Civic Theatre

WILBUR SPARROW
Division of Drama, University of Washington

SAMUEL FRENCH
NEW YORK LOS ANGELES
SAMUEL FRENCH LTD. LONDON

PRINTED IN THE UNITED STATES OF AMERICA
BY THE VAIL-BALLOU PRESS, INC., BINGHAMTON, N. Y.

THE IMAGINED CHARACTER OF ANOTHER

"The essence of poetic art is being able to get outside one's self, to stand apart, study and draw that other self, the imagined character of another, for the eyes and brain of the outside world of men and women to see and know."

from *Robert Browning: Essays and Thoughts*
by John T. Nettleship

ACKNOWLEDGMENTS

THE authors of this book are grateful for the co-operation of Prof. Glenn Hughes, Dr. Erwin A. Esper, Prof. Florence Bean James, Prof. O. B. Sperlin, Dr. Edward Wagenknecht, Mr. Arthur Weinstein, Miss Helen Clare Nelson, Miss Virginia Vogt, Miss Theora Bartholomew, and the classes in acting at the University of Washington.

TABLE OF CONTENTS

FOREWORD

It is a pleasure to introduce a book which requires no apology. *Modern Acting: A Manual* has all the reasons for existence a textbook can have.

The recent rise of the amateur and semi-professional theatre to a new level of excellence is the result of a great deal of careful thinking on the part of its directors. Not only careful thinking but the careful application of thinking to the actual problems of theatrical production. And in certain instances theory and practice have been happily wedded.

In the Division of Drama at the University of Washington we have been unusually successful in correlating academic courses in theatrical subjects with our public performances. The fact that we operate two theatres every week of the year is, of course, a tremendous advantage; but no theatre schedule and no number of theatres could guarantee the results we obtain with our actors unless the foundation of theory were sound and complete.

During the past several years our staff has developed a standard of acting among our students which I believe is unsurpassed in the non-professional theatre and which certainly is above that found in many a professional theatre. This belief is shared by several thousand patrons of our theatres, who long ago have ceased to think of our productions as "college plays."

The fundamentals of acting, as taught in our classes, are

compressed clearly and usefully in the pages of this book. The approach and the method are described and illustrated sufficiently so that others may adopt them and profit by them.

As to the authors: Miss Rosenstein and Mr. Sparrow are members of our teaching staff in charge of classes in theatre speech and acting. They are also, respectively, dramatic director and assistant dramatic director of our public theatres, the Penthouse Theatre and the Studio Theatre. Mr. Haydon is one of our graduate students, recently instructor and art director of productions at the University of Oklahoma and now executive director of the Civic Theatre School, Portland, Oregon.

I predict for this manual a long and useful life, and I am happy to have been asked to stand godfather to it.

Glenn Hughes
Executive Director
Division of Drama
University of Washington
Seattle

2 August 1936

MODERN ACTING: A MANUAL

CHAPTER I

INTRODUCTION

It has sometimes been said that the way to learn to act is to act. If this were true, the way to learn to play a Beethoven sonata would be to sit down at the piano and play a Beethoven sonata. The truth of the matter is, however, that the musician does not start with Beethoven, but rather with the study of the notes and simplest scales. The artist's first task is to master his instrument. In the case of the pianist, it is the piano; in the case of the actor, it is himself. Only after he has achieved this self-mastery is an actor ready to interpret a role in a play, for a play may be likened in complexity of form to a sonata.

It is the business of the actor to present to an audience various overt behavior patterns including those which go under the name of emotion. The problem is to present them in each dramatic situation so that they will seem to be appropriate to the situation and to the character. If the ordinary beginner is confronted with the task of reproducing these behavior patterns he is likely to be completely blocked, because every one involves a complex of facial expression, posture, and voice quality. The essential problem, then, reduces itself to the means by which the student or the teacher instructing him is to induce such a complex and integrated simultaneity of processes. One way is to analyze all of the facial, bodily, and vocal expressions that enter into the conventional manifestation of an emotion. Then it would be necessary to train the beginner in each of these part-movements and expressions one by one with the expectation that he will eventually be able to do them all at once in the complete pattern. Such a method has been tried with swimmers. The beginner is told to float. Next he holds onto a bar and learns to move his feet. Then he stands up and learns the necessary hand and arm movements. He is expected to know how to swim once these part-movements are mastered. The result of this method has not proved satisfactory.

The objections to such an approach in acting are, first: it has been found to be pedagogically unsatisfactory; second: in so far as it is successful it leads to highly conventionalized and wooden patterns. An alternative method which we believe to be much more successful pedagogically and to lead to more individualization, plasticity, and naturalness, is to cause the student to practice the reinstatement of past experience. These must have involved the expression of subjective emotion and feeling similar to those called for by the given dramatic situation and character. Of course, because of the limit of past personal experience, it will be frequently necessary to draw on vicarious experience from such sources as literature, painting, sculpture, and other transmitters of knowledge, as well as upon careful observation of the characteristic behavior of others.

There are undoubtedly passages in the following chapters which will sound peculiar to professional psychologists, but we believe that that peculiarity will be largely a matter of terminology. That terminology has been selected less from the point of view of scientific respectability than from its stimulating value for students of drama. The actual procedures which are described here have been arrived at by a long process of trial and error in the practical pedagogical situation of the drama classroom. A parallel is the teaching method for training animals. Although the description of these methods at first reading frequently sounded somewhat bizarre, psychologists have found many practical procedures for which a sound scientific basis can be made out.

Acting a role does not mean learning lines, cues, stage business, and set responses. It means creating the inner life of the character delineated by the playwright. This includes thoughts, sensations, perceptions, and emotions in fluid state, in constant fluctuation. Only when the actor brings into being this inner life—this stream of consciousness of another being—can he be said to be acting creatively. Therefore the following chapters are concerned with a method of acting which stresses the importance of working from within out, or from the inner feeling to the outer manifestation.

No method in the world, however, can in itself enable an individual to become an actor. *An actor must have talent.* Talent is a superior aptitude for expression in a particular medium. This pre-eminence is an endowment; it cannot be artificially acquired.

A talented actor is one who can express in terms of himself the inner life of another individual. He must possess the qualifications of all other artists, such as heightened sensibility, vivid imagination, and the facility to comment on life through a given medium.

The equipment of the trained actor must include, besides these endowments, developed concentration, keen observation, a plastic body, voice and speech adaptability, and a practical knowledge of literature, history, science, and the arts.

When the actor is so equipped, he is said to have technique. Although talent cannot be taught in a classroom, the elements which comprise a technique can be. The purpose of this handbook is to outline in simple terms a method of learning and teaching this technique. It contains definite exercises, explanations, and a practical approach to the art of acting.

CHAPTER II

SENSIBILITY

EVERY normal person has the capacity to see, to hear, to smell, to taste, and to feel. In the actor these five senses must be developed to an acute degree. An actor possesses adequate sensibility when his sense impressions are so keen that they may be recalled at any time. His sensations of yesterday should have been so sharp that they may be re-created today in retrospect.

For example: a year ago the actor cut his finger. In the role which the same actor is called upon to play today he must simulate cutting his finger. To play the part adequately, he must again experience the sensations which were present at the original accident. If these sensations were strong enough they may be re-created in two ways: one, by the recollection of the emotional response; two, by the recollection of the external bodily response. In other words, "What did I *feel* and *think?*" or "What did I *do?*" That which will aid the re-creation further is a combination of "What did I feel and think and do?"

It is comparatively simple to remember the response to a cut finger because a number of the senses were involved: sight, sound, feeling, perhaps even taste and smell. Suppose while cutting bread the person cuts his finger. Assume he reacts in the following manner:

1. He *feels* the sensation of shock resulting from the passing of the knife into the flesh.

2. He jerks the knife away, drops it and *looks* at his finger.

3. He *sees* the cut, the gush of blood on finger and bread.

4. He puts the finger into his mouth.

5. He *tastes* the blood.

6. He *feels* the drawing in the finger, immediately followed by numbness, followed by throbbing.

7. He fears it is a bad cut.

8. He *looks* at the finger, realizing the cut is a bad one.

9. With increasing fear, he calls for help, simultaneously putting his finger under cold water.

10. He *feels* the sting of water on the wound.

11. He *hears* the rush of water and the coming of help.

12. He *sees* his mother, who has answered his call, and at sight of help he experiences momentary relief which is immediately followed by fear of delay.

13. He *sees* his mother take iodine from the cupboard.

14. He anticipates the pain of iodine.

15. He *hears* the uncorking of the bottle.

16. He *smells* iodine.

17. He *feels* the pain of iodine on the wound.

18. He paces until the pain decreases and the iodine dries.

19. Pain ceases, tenseness decreases; he feels exhaustion from the shock of the experience.

The individual, then, has undergone the following sensory experiences:

1. *Feeling* of pain varying from numbness to throbbing.

2. *Sight* of cut, blood, iodine, and surroundings.

3. *Taste* of blood.

4. *Smell* of blood, iodine.

5. *Sound* of falling knife, the rush of water, and the approach of help.

Now the actor is faced with the problem of simulating the above event. What are his thought processes? First, he recalls his dominant sensation; thus if *taste* of blood brought forth his keenest reaction, he will recollect it first. From that point he reconstructs the previous and following sensations. Once the whole experience is re-created, he may organize his thought processes into the original order.

Even slighter experiences, those which involve the responses of only one sense, such as the sight of a tall building, the sound of a mouse scratching, or the smell of rain, should leave indelible impressions. After our first contacts we are prone to accept these minor responses as a matter of course. The actor, however, must be once again cognizant of them in order to record them mentally and store them up for future use. An actor must remember that habitual acceptance of the world around him dulls his perception and thus becomes his deadliest enemy.

The following exercises are suggested to develop the senses.

Exercise I

The student should be required to keep a diary in which he records some of his predominant sense reactions of the day.

For example: the shock of a door which was slammed, the smell of an apple pie cooking, the feel of icy streets, the taste of sulphur fumes in a chemistry laboratory, and the sight of the sun shining through a window on the pages of a book.

Exercise II

The teacher produces an object, such as a small earthenware pitcher, and allows the student to handle it for one minute. (This means one minute for each member in the class, but one person should not observe another person while that individual is examining the object.) When a student has finished the allotted observation period he describes in writing the object he has just handled. This writing period should last from three to four minutes. If he has seen the mere exterior, commenting on only the color, shape, and height, his perception is defective. If in feeling the pitcher he has had no new experience his sense of touch is undeveloped, for few objects are exactly alike.

This exercise with new objects should be repeated until a complete and accurate description of each object is obtained. Such a description should include shape, proportion, color, composition, texture, quality of construction, functions, defects and an association through comparison and contrast with other objects and experiences.

For example: the pitcher is made of clay, proportioned only slightly taller than it is wide, of mottled green-brown and orange color, a smooth texture marred by flecks of sand, crudely constructed, intended to be used as a cream pitcher for tea service, and marred by slight chips on the rim. Among possible associations are the shape and coloring of a bean pot, the peasant handwork such as the Mexican olla for cooling water, and a handle which suggests ribbon candy in its flat wide curl. On rubbing the pitcher one feels surprise at the combination of smoothness and roughness due to the glaze covering rough flecks, and at the feeling of fragileness in connection with an earthenware object.

Exercise III

When Exercise II has been completed the student is asked to improvise a character which contains the qualities found in the pitcher.

For example: the pitcher may have suggested a short fat peasant woman with a load of bound kindling twigs on her shoulders. The color suggests items of costume and disposition. The interpretations differ according to the experience and imagination of the students executing them, but they should portray the quintessence of the pitcher. The improvisation should not contain the use of the actual article.

Exercise IV

The teacher says, "Visualize the following: the ocean the first time you saw it, a tall building, your favorite armchair." He names any number of other objects.

In giving this exercise, the teacher should use examples which are actual and not imaginary, because they must be in the direct experience of the student. Watch carefully the changes in body and facial expression as the student becomes immersed in the recollection.

Exercise V

Two notes are sounded. The student is asked to distinguish which is higher in pitch. This drill must be repeated many times in one session and in a number of sessions until the student gives the answer quickly and accurately.

Exercise VI

A military air, such as *Stars and Stripes Forever,* is played. Students must describe their reactions as to the satisfaction or dissatisfaction, as to the quality of performance, as to the rhythm, tempo, and personal association.

For example: the student dislikes the tune, points out discords, discovers a tendency in himself to beat out time, and visualizes soldiers marching.

Exercise VII

Improvise a character suggested by the military march. This may be a pompous disciplinarian in a summer camp, who moves with short regular steps and speaks with a rough voice.

Exercise VIII

1. Recall the sound of an aeroplane passing over your house; describe it in detail. Test your description by listening carefully to the next aeroplane you actually hear.

2. Recall the sound of a starting automobile; describe it in detail. Test your description by listening carefully to the next automobile you hear start.

3. Recall the sound of dance music. In this exercise the teacher should watch very carefully the reaction of face and body of the student.

4. Recall the purring of a cat. Here again the teacher should watch facial and body response.

The teacher should observe and point out the physical reactions to the class. As the group improve they may observe one another.

Exercise IX

Bring to class a flower which has a strong odor. Pass it around and have the class describe it. Compare notes. An adequate answer should tell whether the odor is pleasant or unpleasant, sweet or spicy, lingering or fleeting, delicate or heavy, and the associations the odor brings forth.

For example: the odor of carnation is pleasant, spicy and lingering, and heavy. Its association may be with a funeral parlor or with graduation.

Exercise X

Improvise a character suggested by the carnation.

For example: a stolid middle-class housewife who may be depended upon for a well-run, clean, refreshing house. The color of the carnation will no doubt change the character somewhat.

Exercise XI

Pass around a bag of lemon drops and have the class describe the taste of the candy. An adequate description should tell whether it is pleasant or unpleasant, sweet or sour, mild or strong, and should give its associations.

For example: a lemon drop is pleasant, sweet until the coating has dissolved, then sour and fairly strong, and a possible association is the corner candy store near the grammar school.

Exercise XII

Improvise a character suggested by a lemon drop.

For example: a prim, not unattractive-looking spinster who has a fixed smile and a vigorous walk.

The foregoing exercises are designed mainly to intensify sense impressions. They might also be called exercises in *concentration*. If the student at the end of a long practice period has learned to see or to hear with exactness and thoroughness so that no detail has escaped him, there is no doubt that he has developed what we call *concentration*. Without it, it is impossible to give uninterrupted attention to the analysis of anything. However, we shall not treat *concentration* as a separate problem. We assume here that it is a necessary but unconscious accompaniment of that painstaking analysis which we are stressing in regard to observation and sensibility.

We emphasize the importance of sense impressions because the stronger the sensations connected with the incident, the easier it is to recall the accompanying emotions. Richard Boleslavsky says, "We have a special memory for feelings which works unconsciously by itself and for itself." It is more familiar to some of us as "conditioned response."

For example: if at the first Junior Prom a girl attends, the dance begins with the *Merry Widow Waltz,* it is very likely that the music of the *Merry Widow Waltz* when heard later in life will recall the surroundings and emotions of that evening. As the memory grows dimmer the music may recall to her only a vague feeling of satisfaction. The exact circumstances may fade altogether, but always the unconscious pleasant reaction will remain.

If in our present acting problem we are striving for a certain emotion, *how exactly do we go about recalling a complete incident that contained that emotion?*

Suppose an actress must play the following scene. The setting is a park; the time, a summer night. She and her fiancé are seated on a park bench. They are planning their wedding. Her feeling should be one of mingled pleasure, anticipation, and satisfaction. The actress looks back into her experience for similar feelings. She recalls the Junior Prom. The recollection is vague and hazy until she remembers a definite sense response, which in this case happens to be *hearing* the music of the *Merry Widow Waltz*. She then unconsciously calls to mind the strains of the piece and with that recollection come suggestions of the presence of her partner, the color of her dress. All the accompanying feelings and actions of the event one by one return. Forcing herself to listen to the imaginary *Merry Widow Waltz,* she has re-experienced the emotions which belonged to her earlier experience, the Junior Prom. She has the further problem now of transferring these emotions, re-created through remembrance, to the girl sitting in the park on a happy occasion. In order to transfer them she uses more than *sensibility*. Here she calls upon *imagination* as well, but it is important to remember that it was the sense impression on which she depended first. The manner in which *imagination* intensifies and magnifies a primary sensation or emotion we shall understand more fully later.

If the actress were able to hear the actual music of the *Merry Widow Waltz* and from hearing it found her thoughts returning to her early experience, she would be undergoing a "conditioned response." Unfortunately in the theatre no such convenience is possible. The actress must imagine the music and respond to its fictitious strains. She must use the intangible memory of a strong sensation as a stimulus to start a response. Therefore the stronger the sensation the more easily the entire emotion may be recalled. The sensations are the keys to emotions.

In this system of *memory of emotion* through directed recollection the teacher should stress that not only the early sensations should be recalled but also all the physical details, all the actions which accompanied the event.

For example: in recalling the dance, the actress remembers that she smiled at her partner, that when they stopped for a moment between pieces she wiped the moisture from her right hand with her handkerchief, which she held in her left hand. By going through this action it might be possible to call up the emotional reaction. It is true, no doubt, that sometimes an actor will start his process of recollection with a physical movement instead of a sensation. Perhaps the actress has the following experience: whenever she sees another person wipe moisture from one hand with the other, the moment on the dance floor flashes through her mind. Thus she goes through the act when she wants to recall deliberately the emotional response of the moment. The sensations, then, follow the body response. To have a complete and comparatively reliable recollection of the incident, whether the actor starts with a recollected sensation or with a recollected action, it is to his advantage to finish with a complete picture. This must include physical as well as emotional responses.

The question arises as to whether an actor must go through this elaborate process for every feeling which may be contained in the part throughout the play. If a beginning actor had such a role, the answer would be yes. It is true, however, that the more skilled an actor becomes the less he has to do *consciously* to recall his early emotions. The associations between the present feeling and the earlier one will take place with little conscious effort. But in the first rehearsals even the trained actor finds that recollection of specific experience clarifies action and feeling in the portrayal of his new role. As the rehearsals progress, he will find that the proper emotions in the right degree of intensity now appear in response to the particular circumstances of the present play. Fewer and fewer of the details of the original experience need be recalled.

It is also true that these recollected sensations and emotions will not in themselves be strong enough to create the new emotion in its full realization. Again *memory of emotion* must be supplemented by imagination.

Exercise XIII

The student is given the following problems. Using the classroom setting as his stage and his own self as the character, he recalls for each statement an early experience. This should be done aloud and in detail.

For example: the student is asked to say just the two words, "It's hot." She looks into her past, selects a particular experience of heat and describes it aloud. "I was sitting on a deck chair of an ocean liner last June when I went to Europe with my family. It was three o'clock in the afternoon. I was wearing a white linen tennis dress with a jacket. A bandana handkerchief was tied around my head. I had no stockings but was wearing beach sandals. I must have dozed for fifteen or twenty minutes. When I awoke, my whole body seemed to be covered with perspiration. My dress was limp and clung to me. I felt completely enervated and my eyes ached from the sunlight. I pulled off the bandana and sat up slowly. I removed my jacket. As I did this I turned to a woman beside me and said, 'I don't think I can stand this heat much longer.'"

After this oral résumé, the student should take time to go over the entire process again in silence. If she is still unable to recall her sensation she may have to repeat the oral and the silent procedure again and again until it is more thoroughly realized. Now with the sensation more clearly perceived she recalls the experience once more silently and says aloud at the right moment, "It's hot."

Exercises

1. It's hot.
2. It's cold.
3. I'm frightened.
4. I'm tired.
5. I'm sick.
6. I'm bored.
7. I'm happy.
8. I'm nervous.
9. I hate him.
10. How still it is!
11. What a relief!
12. Leave me alone.

CHAPTER III

OBSERVATION

OBSERVATION is the faculty of recognizing and noting. It is the means by which the actor contacts and analyzes the world about him. These contacts are made through the senses: sight, smell, taste, touch, and sound. But there is more to observation than sense response. There may be a possible emotional response and an intellectual one.

For example: we *look* at a rose. It is our *sense of sight* that has made the *contact.* If the rose is *associated* with any kind of memory, such as a wedding, a party, or a graduation, it may stimulate an *emotional reaction.* If we *analyze* the rose to any extent, as to color, quality, texture, or condition, we have made an *intellectual comment.*

Thus the process of observation may be divided into three parts: sense response, emotional response, and intellectual response.

Since we have discussed sense response and its development in the foregoing chapter, we shall devote little time to it here. Nor shall we concern ourselves now with emotional response, which is discussed more fittingly under such headings as sensibility, imagination, the actor's medium, and concentration. Our emphasis here is upon the element of observation which we call *intellectual response.*

How exactly can this observation process be described?

For example: we are seated in a crowded restaurant. We

glance casually about the room. We are *contacting* everything that meets our eyes, ears, nose, taste, and touch. No doubt we are registering everything we encounter. We have not brought our attention to rest on anything specific until an interesting face at a near-by table catches our eyes. In *watching* the face we are amused by certain expressions and we laugh. This *emotional response* conveyed to us through sight is wholly unconscious. Now, however, we force ourselves to study the face. We *analyze* it. We are making an *intellectual comment.* We discover that the eyes are deep set, the nose is bulbous and at a peculiar angle to the face, and the teeth are spread. Through association of ideas, we place the owner of the face as to type.

The following exercises are designed to strengthen the power of analysis or the intellectual response.

The first group deals with accuracy, for the actor must be exact in recording in his mind the details he has observed, and he must be exact in reproducing them for an audience.

For example: the student is asked to sharpen a pencil in pantomime. He uses no actual properties. The teacher and students watch the procedure and discuss his proficiency. He then is given a pencil and a knife and actually sharpens the pencil. A comparison is made between the two procedures. His accuracy of pantomime is checked. This method is followed in the next group of exercises.

Exercise I

1. Make a telephone call.
2. Shine a shoe.
3. Handle a teacup.
4. Open and close a door.

5. Remove a coat.
6. Write a letter, seal, and stamp it.
7. Comb and brush the hair.
8. Erase a blackboard.
9. Read and fold a newspaper.
10. Spin a top.
11. Wind and set a clock.
12. Play jacks.
13. Shuffle and deal cards.
14. Darn a sock.
15. Beat an egg.
16. Wipe the hands.
17. Light and smoke a cigarette.
18. Turn and cut the leaves of a new book.
19. Take a snapshot with a kodak.
20. Try on a hat.

The second group of exercises involves re-enactment of scenes and the testing of their accuracy. On the previous day the student has been assigned specific actions. They are to be done actually and analyzed before class. Now the process is reproduced in pantomime.

For example: the student is assigned to set the table at home. He now re-enacts this scene in class. The students and teacher watch him and check his accuracy from their previous experience.

Exercise II

1. Re-enact packing a trunk or suitcase.
2. Re-enact cleaning a room.
3. Re-enact making a bed.
4. Re-enact cutting a watermelon or other seasonal fruit.

5. Re-enact building a fire in a fireplace.
6. Re-enact eating breakfast.
7. Re-enact selecting a book from the library.
8. Re-enact making a purchase.
9. Re-enact washing your hair.
10. Re-enact pressing a garment.
11. Re-enact typing a letter.
12. Re-enact setting a table for a dinner party.
13. Re-enact stroking an animal.
14. Re-enact making-up for the street or stage.
15. Re-enact hanging a picture.
16. Re-enact re-arranging furniture in a room.
17. Re-enact examining an empty stage.
18. Re-enact a visit to a museum.
19. Re-enact a visit to a park.
20. Re-enact a visit to a theatre.

So far this observation has been directed to ourselves. We now turn our attention to the behavior patterns of others.

For example: we watch a man eat soup. Tomorrow in the classroom we reproduce his exact movements. While a comment is made on the character by reproducing his actions, the stress is not on characterization, but rather on detail, such as which fingers were uppermost in holding the spoon, how quickly he refilled the spoon, and how he handled his napkin.

Exercise III

1. Watch some one arrange flowers in a vase.
2. Watch some one dust a room.
3. Watch some one drive a car.
4. Watch some one listen to a salesman.

5. Watch some one make a purchase.
6. Watch a barber cut hair.
7. Watch some one eat luncheon.
8. Watch some one get on and settle himself in a street-car.
9. Watch some one teach a class.
10. Watch some one cook a meal.
11. Watch a shoemaker mend a shoe.
12. Watch a musician play a musical instrument.
13. Watch a concert artist make an entrance.
14. Watch a child at play.
15. Watch a worker in a factory.
16. Watch a mechanic at work.
17. Watch a nurse at work.
18. Watch a hairdresser at work.
19. Watch a beggar on the street.
20. Watch a doorman at a hotel.

The foregoing exercises were designed to teach the student to register accurately the important details of all of the material he encounters. It is not enough, however, that he records an increased number of random impressions. His senses, which serve as messengers from the outer world to his inner consciousness, should be messengers which are directed to select the richest and most valuable material for the actor.

For example: through his sense of sight, keenly developed after extensive drill as prescribed in the foregoing chapter, he observes an unfamiliar living-room. He notes the number of details in the room, such as yellow walls, soft green rug, and a brown brocaded Duncan Phyfe davenport. If his sensibilities have not been heightened he will have nothing but a general impression of a well-furnished living-room. Let us assume, however, that he exhausts each article in the room. It is now our problem to select from these articles any that may be of special importance to the actor. What he selects for further attention must be something of extraordinary value to store up in his experience. For instance, in this room is an antique Chippendale mirror which in design and connotation is an article of historic and aesthetic value. It speaks of another period, calls to mind men and women of another era; it may even suggest a particular scene. For the actor this piece has unusual significance and deserves added attention even though the cursory examination took in its outward details thoroughly.

The first concrete step in the development of selectivity is to discover what constituents in the surrounding world can be utilized most effectively by the actor.

There are certain definite methods by which an actor may be qualified to exercise judgment. He must, of course, be widely read and extensively informed in fields of education and culture. There are certain exercises which will enable him to utilize immediately the significant elements of life and literature which are already a part of his experience.

The following exercises are designed to stimulate observation of material especially valuable to the actor.

For example: the students as a class go to the public market; they walk carefully through the market place observing the people and activity around them. At the next class meeting each student re-enacts the character that made the deepest impression upon him. The stress again is not upon characterization but rather upon the exactness of gesture, movement, and all other visible manifestations.

If the student recalls a fruit vendor who stood with forearms folded beneath a voluminous apron that was tied around his waist, he assumes the posture and movements of that person.

Exercise IV

1. Go to a depot.
2. Go to the waterfront.
3. Go to a factory.
4. Go to a nursery school.
5. Go to a hospital.
6. Go to a prison.
7. Go to a court.
8. Go to a concert.
9. Go to a lecture.
10. Go to a bread line.
11. Go to an amusement park.
12. Go to a wedding.
13. Go to a funeral.
14. Go to a political meeting.
15. Go to a religious street-meeting.
16. Go to a dance.
17. Go to the theatre.
18. Go to church.
19. Go to any foreign section of the city.
20. Go to an art museum.

In the following group of exercises the process is reversed. The student selects a character for whom he desires more specific mannerisms. Thereupon he goes to the place where he would be most likely to find similar characters. At the next class meeting he adapts those mannerisms to the chosen character. If the student is interested in such a person as a minister, he visits several churches and from his observation of a number of clergymen selects behavior which is characteristic of the particular person he has in mind.

Exercise V

1. Choose a doctor.
2. Choose a lawyer.
3. Choose a clerk.
4. Choose a floor-walker.
5. Choose a waiter.
6. Choose a bootblack.
7. Choose a mechanic.
8. Choose a factory worker.
9. Choose a streetcar conductor.
10. Choose an insurance salesman.
11. Choose an artist.
12. Choose a newsboy.
13. Choose a typist.
14. Choose a beggar.
15. Choose a peddler.
16. Choose a political office-holder.
17. Choose a concert singer.
18. Choose a policeman.
19. Choose a school teacher.
20. Choose a dance orchestra leader.
21. Choose a torch singer.
22. Choose a soda jerker.
23. Choose a loafer.
24. Choose a cigar-store clerk.
25. Choose a cashier at a bank.

26. Choose a janitor.
27. Choose a butler.
28. Choose a male hairdresser.
29. Choose an unemployed worker.
30. Choose a soap-box orator.

The question arises, would not the above exercises lead to pure imitation? If the teacher or student were satisfied to end his study with a perfect reproduction of the details observed, with no further attention upon why they were made and what their exact relationship was to the mental and emotional make-up of the individuals involved, a charge of mimicry would be justified. To avoid sheer imitation, then, it is important that the teacher and student discover the possible motivation of every mannerism observed. The student may not be adroit enough yet to unite successfully the observed physical details with their motivation, but he should be able to record these things accurately, in order to store them up for the time when he will be able to create a complete character. It should be kept in mind that no reproduction, no matter how accurate, may be called a re-creation until it is the direct expression of the inner consciousness.

All suggested material for observation has been taken from life rather than from other actors. We feel that it is of primary importance to the actor to go directly to his sources of inspiration and information, rather than to the second-hand usage of it which other actors have already made. Suggestions from other actors may be helpful, but these should be received as a bibliography is received from other scholars.

CHAPTER IV

IMAGINATION

ALL theorists are agreed that imagination is a primary requisite of the actor. The word *imagination* implies creative power, a power which enables us to have *ideal* experience. Ideal in this case refers to mental as opposed to actual. To conceive of such an experience which we have not actually undergone does not mean that that experience is entirely fictitious. More often than not it is possible to trace these mental images to earlier reactions.

For example: the child imagines he sees a camel in a cloud at which he is looking. He has linked with the cloud the shape of a toy camel with which he has played.

Sometimes it is more difficult to trace these associations because the fundamental element may exist in what we often refer to as the subconscious. The inability to recognize the element in this picture by means of past experience may be called *fantasy* by some. However, we believe that this fantasy is traceable, and a fuller discussion of this will be given later.

Every experience in life is recorded in the human being. Nothing is entirely lost. It is true that many of these experiences are too slight to be recalled as easily as the camel was for the child. Nevertheless, they may at some time play an important part in our later life.

For example: the actor must play the part of a dying man.

Obviously, he has no actual former experience to draw upon, yet he maintains that his feelings are authentic. He says he is depending on his imagination. But is it not true that his imagination is depending on such former experiences as complete exhaustion, difficulty in catching his breath, fainting, falling asleep, or taking an anaesthetic? Even if the actor has not used these reactions consciously as he did in the exercises in the first chapter, nevertheless they are active in his creation of this new concept. Thus these reactions can become elements in a new picture which he may have been convinced was a figment of imagination.

If the actor is to play a dying man as in the example above, he is not depending on sheer imagination. He is depending on *memory of emotion* as well. But if he is to play a particular kind of dying man, say a very old man, under particular circumstances, such as death from lack of water on a desert island, then he is forced to transfer this memory of emotions to the new circumstances. It is in this act of transferring that imagination plays its part.

For example: the actress has the following problem. She is playing the role of Ase in *Peer Gynt;* it is the scene in which she dies. The particular circumstances are: Ase is old, worried for Peer's safety, happy to have him with her, in pain, uncomfortable in the cramping quarters of the small bed which belonged to Peer as a child. At moments she is transported into the dream world that Peer creates for her as he weaves the story of the ride to St. Peter. Her attention is broken, however, now by pain, now by fright at approaching death. In the final moments she is weakened by the emotional strain; she falls back limply against the bed and says to Peer, "I'll lie back then and trust me to you, my boy." Let us take the problems of interpretation in this scene.

From her own *memory* she draws this:

1. The actress recalls her severest illness and her weakest moments.

2. She recalls the relief of relying on the nurse present.

3. She recalls the satisfaction of having her mother beside her.

4. She recalls another time when she sat in a crowded automobile for hours at a time.

5. She remembers the pain of a burn received from hot sealing wax.

6. She recalls the fear of endangering her mother's health through her own illness.

7. She recalls her childish absorption in fairy tales.

From her *observation* she draws the following:

1. The picture of old age.

2. Norwegian characteristics.

3. The furnishings of the room.

It will take her *imagination,* however, to:

1. Intensify the feelings accompanying illness, weakness, and pain that she is actually able to recall.

2. To visualize the person, the feelings and the circumstances as one.

3. To transfer all these experiences to the character.

4. To believe in the result as truth.

This process, which is one of *intensification, visualization, assimilation,* and *conviction,* is imagination.

It is apparent, then, that a vivid imagination is one that can intensify emotions, can inject these emotions into a given pattern, can visualize physical aspects and can believe the composite.

How can such an imagination be developed?

In the preceding chapters we learned the importance of associating the emotions we are trying to arouse with actual experience. Once we recall a former emotion we must sustain it long enough to transpose it to the new situation. To do this adequately, we must no longer think of the circumstances which accompanied the real experience. What actually happened in the incident that we are recalling is of no further use to us once the emotion is recalled. We needed those actions only to help us restore the sensations or emotion of the moment. Now that we have re-experienced those sensations we want them to accompany only the new situation. In the words of the psychologist we are substituting new stimuli to arouse a similar reaction. It is not easy to dispense with these recollected details. They may prove troublesome by intruding on the new picture. It is only by constant drill that we can learn to drop them at will and preserve only the emotion they served to revive.

For example: a student in the class had the problem of portraying fear of a man awaiting execution in a dungeon. The most outstanding example of impending terror which he was able to recall occurred when he was a child. He was awaiting a dreaded whipping from his father. The student had no difficulty in re-experiencing terror, but when he attempted to transfer it to the dungeon situation he found such details as the nature of the room of his childhood home and the vision of his father intruding themselves into his consciousness. What should have happened is this:

1. He recalls such details as
   a. hearing his father making preparations in the next room,
   b. dryness in his mouth, and
   c. seeing the door through which his father will come.
2. From these he is able to re-create the emotion of fear.
3. He must center his attention on the general feeling of fear and its manifestations to such an extent that that emotion dominates him. The details which helped him recall it are forgotten for the moment in the intensity of the new stress.
4. Now with that feeling still strong within him the student goes on with the action in the dungeon. The important thing is to continue the new action at the moment when he experiences fear rather than at the moment when he is involved in the mechanics of re-creating fear.

The following exercises are intended as drill to heighten the imagination. All the exercises in this chapter should be repeated over a long period of time. The form should be retained, but new material introduced by the teacher and the development of the facility to imagine noted.

The problems are to be done in pantomime; the entire class should participate in all of them. The teacher divides the time allotted to each exercise into two parts. During the first period the students recall specific personal experiences involving the general emotional reaction to be stressed. During the second period they apply the general reaction to the new given circumstances. The division should come when the teacher feels the students have had time to complete the mechanics and to re-experience the sensation or emotion. A pencil tap may mark the end of the first period.

For example: the word "fatigue" is given to the class as a problem. The feeling is to be applied to a factory worker whose job is to sew buttons on men's vests as fast as the garments are passed to him from the next worker. It is six o'clock in the evening after a ten-hour day. The students sit silently for the first period, each recalling a personal experience of fatigue. When sensations such as muscular aches in the fingers, back, and legs, and the feeling of mental stagnation become dominant, the student goes directly into the action of sewing imaginary buttons on imaginary vests. While he does not rise from his seat he will probably shift position from the relaxed one that he has assumed as he underwent the recollection to one which will enable him to accomplish the task described.

The teacher, through his observation of facial change and small movements of the body, will soon be able to detect the right moment for marking the change from one period to another.

Exercise I

1. Heat. Recall an experience of heat. Improvise a scene in which you are seated at a band concert, the sun blazing upon you, the music temporarily stopped. You are fanning yourself with a program and drinking tepid soda water.

2. Cold. Recall an experience of cold. Improvise a scene in which you are playing the scales on a piano in a room in which all heat has been cut off at a time of zero weather.

3. Pain. Recall an experience of pain. Improvise a scene in which you are sitting at a table eating dinner with your family. All the time your head is throbbing from eye strain, a discomfort you are attempting to hide from your family.

4. Boredom. Recall an experience of boredom. Improvise a scene in which you are in prison. You are seated at a bench tacking heels onto shoes. You have done this job daily for a year.

5. Pleasure. Recall an experience of pleasure. Improvise a scene in which you open a box which contains a watch you have bought that afternoon.

6. Regret. Recall an experience of regret. Improvise a scene in which you are opening a box which contains a watch you have bought that afternoon. On your way home, after buying the watch you saw another you liked better than the one you are examining.

7. Relaxation. Recall an experience of relaxation. Improvise a scene in which you are on a boat on a trip to Europe after a busy season in New York. You are stretched out on a deck chair in the warmth of the sun with no worries and a pleasant vacation ahead of you.

8. Revenge. Recall an experience of revenge. Improvise a scene in an office in which you are writing a letter of discharge to a fellow clerk who has lied about you to your mutual employer.

9. Fear. Recall an experience of fear. Improvise a scene in which you are sitting in the waiting-room of a doctor's office. You have just had an examination for tuberculosis and you are awaiting the verdict.

10. Fatigue. Recall an experience of fatigue. Improvise a scene in which you are wrapping Christmas presents in a booth in a department store. It is nearly closing time on the day before Christmas and the store has stayed open until late in the evening.

The second group of exercises, also intended to intensify emotion, entails more action. They should be done separately by members of the class in pantomime. The same timing method should be used by the teacher.

Exercise II

1. Heat. Recall an experience of heat. Improvise a scene in which you are typing in an office on the warmest day of summer. You walk to the window for relief but find the air outside even warmer than inside. You stop for a glass of water and return to your typewriter.

2. Cold. Recall an experience of cold. Improvise a scene in which you are driving a car on the coldest day of the year. The car stops and you get out and examine the radiator, which is frozen. You attempt to hail passing cars, at the same time trying to keep active to fight the cold.

3. Pain. Recall an experience of pain. Improvise a scene in which you get a toothache in the middle of the night. You get out of bed, go to the medicine cabinet, and, finding no remedy, you pace the floor in agony.

4. Boredom. Recall an experience of boredom. Improvise a scene in which you have been practicing on the piano for an hour. You pick up the clock and find you have fifteen minutes more to practice.

5. Pleasure. Recall an experience of pleasure. Improvise a scene in which you are packing your clothes to leave for the seashore.

6. Regret. Recall an experience of regret. Improvise a scene in which you are packing your clothes to return home after an all too short week-end.

7. Relaxation. Recall an experience of relaxation. Improvise a scene in which you have been studying at a desk all evening. You get up, go into the other room, turn on the radio, and do anything you are accustomed to do for relaxation.

8. Revenge. Recall an experience of revenge. Improvise a scene in which you search for, find, and destroy the manuscript which represents the life work of an enemy.

9. Fear. Recall an experience of fear. Improvise a scene in which you are in a room to which a madman is trying to gain admittance.

10. Fatigue. Recall an experience of fatigue. Improvise a scene in which you are scrubbing floors and washing windows.

The foregoing exercises and discussions have stressed changes of feeling within the actor. Emotions and sensations were brought to life with the help of *vision*. We *visualized* mechanical details which helped to reproduce psychic reactions. When the psychic reaction or emotional response was at its strongest we utilized it in a new set of circumstances. To create these new circumstances we called upon *vision* once again; this time we had to *visualize* new surroundings which had no actual reality in our direct memory. These new surroundings may be likened to the particular demands of the setting the playwright has prescribed. It was comparatively easy to visualize the circumstances which surrounded the real experience we first drew upon, because we had memory on which to rely. Now, however, we must build a picture which has no such definite basis.

For example: in the problem of the dungeon and its effects, the student has the recollection of the room in which he had the spanking, and the sight of his father. This recollection was comparatively easy because it existed in fact at one time. When the emotion was started in full he kept it in mind and maintained it at the same time that he visualized the setting of the dungeon. Now this second time that he calls upon vision he encounters difficulty, for now he has no fact on which to draw. He must produce out of thin air, as it were, this present scene of the dungeon.

This process of *visualizing* is included in what we call imagination. It is demanded then of the actor that he construct these pictures accurately and easily.

His accuracy will depend upon his power of observation, his facility will depend upon the amount of his experience. Both observation and experience can be controlled; observation can be developed in several ways, as we have already demonstrated. *Facility* and *speed* in vision can be acquired. One conscious method of developing them is by drill.

In the following exercises the student is given a word and told to say the word, using visualization in connection with it. After he has said the word he is allowed to visualize a particular association with it. Then he is to repeat the word with that particular connection in mind. Each student should do each one in the prescribed manner.

For example: the word *lamp* is given to the student. The student repeats the word with no particular lamp in mind. Then he is told to visualize a certain lamp. After a moment he repeats the word. If he has visualized an Aladdin's Lamp the intonation and expression of the word will differ from the interpretation he might give had he visualized an ordinary study lamp.

Exercise III

1. Infant.
2. Schoolboy.
3. Lover.
4. Soldier.
5. Middle-aged judge.
6. Old man.
7. Rose.
8. Sunset.
9. Ocean.
10. Mountain.
11. Aeroplane.
12. Wayside inn.
13. Radio.
14. Church.
15. Actor.
16. Boat.
17. Statue.
18. Island.
19. Animal.
20. King.

The next exercises should be timed; three minutes for the concoction of the picture, four minutes for writing the description. The entire class should participate and the results should be read aloud and discussed.

For example: picture the Grand Throne Room of Kublai Khan in Cathay. After a three-minute interval the student writes, giving himself four minutes to get the impression on paper. When read aloud, the description may sound like this: "I see a long narrow room with a wall covered with small, richly colored patterns, like that on a cloisonné vase. The colors are largely gold, green, and blue, with a border of thin red lines. Lavish rugs of jade green and gold cover the floor. The ceilings are shaped like those of a Chinese temple. On the left of the throne are three large windows shaped like entrances to pagodas. Through these can be seen dazzling sunshine on full-blossomed trees. The Khan, in robes of blue, heavily brocaded, is seated on the throne, his knees spread, his hands hidden in the folds of his voluminous sleeves. He wears long conventional mustachios. On his head is a black satin cap with the usual mandarin's button. He is the only person seated in the room. The throne is mounted on an elevation three steps high; these are also carpeted. At the foot of the steps stand three ambassadors from the provinces, dressed in less finery but in interesting colors of yellows, reds, and greens. All attention is turned, not upon the Khan, but on the heavy double doors of hammered bronze at the opposite end of the room. These doors are in the process of opening and there is a feeling of expectancy in the room in anticipation of the entrance of the Princess."

Although the above description depends a good deal on observation, it is not likely that the student relied directly and solely upon it. He has probably never seen such a room either on the stage or in life. He may be familiar with many elements from reading and sight, but the exact combination is new. Although, then, this exercise is to some extent a test in observation, it is primarily a problem in quick visualization.

EXERCISE IV

1. Picture the tomb of an Egyptian king.
2. Picture the dining-room of King Arthur.
3. Picture Noah's Ark.
4. Picture Daniel in the lions' den.
5. Picture the inside of a rocket ship.
6. Picture a Turkish bazaar.
7. Picture a native hut in the midst of an African jungle.
8. Picture the inside of a sea grotto.
9. Picture Cleopatra's barge.
10. Picture the camp of Caesar.

The following problems are designed to preserve realistic detail but to change the exact proportions. While they tax the imagination a little further than the foregoing exercises, they still have some basis in familiar reality. In these exercises the student walks around in the scene he has created, pointing out and describing aloud each object he encounters. He does not, however, handle these objects. Three minutes should be taken before starting, in which the student constructs the scene silently to himself.

EXERCISE V

1. A Lilliputian kitchen.
2. The living-room of a giant.
3. A miniature ocean liner.
4. A gigantic automobile.
5. A room of "distortion" mirrors.

In the foregoing chapter on observation the student was given simple problems of handling objects with which he was familiar in everyday life. Now he is to see and use those objects in a manner which he would not ordinarily employ.

For example: cutting a watermelon. This time he is asked to cut a watermelon with a spoon. In this drill he has the added problem of his unfamiliarity with the action, the incongruity of circumstances, and the effect on himself of the dilemma.

Exercise VI

1. Sew a button on with your left hand.
2. Bail out a boat with a leaky bucket.
3. Walk through a door backward.
4. Comb your hair with a toothpick.
5. Write a letter with burnt matches.
6. Warm your hands on a cigar-lighter.
7. Peel an apple with scissors.
8. Open a can with a hammer.
9. Sweep the floor with a whisk broom.
10. Dig a trench with a small tin can.

In the next exercise an object is passed around the room to be handled as if it were a kitten.

Exercise VII

1. Assume the block of wood is a Pekingese.
2. Assume the block of wood is a baby.
3. Assume the block of wood is a watermelon.
4. Assume the block of wood is a bowl of soup.
5. Assume the block of wood is a piece of ice.

We said that facility and speed in visualization can be developed. We suggested time drills as one method of development. A second method is by increasing *vicarious experience.* We mean by *vicarious experience* insight into the performance and reactions of another gained by unconscious association of yourself with the doings of the performer. Any knowledge from reading, observation of others, and from hearsay would be included in this category.

> *For example:* the actor then is given the problem of playing the part of a man shipwrecked on a desert island. In searching through his experience he recalls his feelings while reading *Robinson Crusoe.*

It is characteristic of us to lose ourselves in the people whom we read of in a book or see in the theatre. Out of this temporary absorption comes valuable material. Without our knowing, we have followed the thoughts, feelings, and actions of other human beings carefully and deeply. There is a certain definite wisdom derived from this process. We have entered the lives of people about us and lived with them long enough to understand their actions and experience their sensations. It is true that our feeling for them is not so strong as our own emotional reaction. However, when we have left their lives—the book is closed, the play ended, the story over—we return to ourselves with new insight and illumination, and, as actors, with new material.

In acquiring this new material a special process has intensified our receptivity. This feeling which we have for the characters we are watching or reading about is stronger than sympathy; it involves not *feeling with* some one, but *feeling as* some one. It is *empathy.*

> *For example:* I see in the moving picture, *Modern Times,* Charlie Chaplin skating unknowingly on the edge of a balcony that has no railing. Each time he approaches the

edge I have the sensation of myself approaching the edge of the balcony, any minute to be plunged over the brink. I find myself suppressing screams of fear and excitement. At the moment I am living and feeling with the character. This feeling is *empathy*.

Again: I am visiting a classroom. A boy rises to recite. He is unable to think of the answer. Although the problem is not mine, I suffer with him. This is more than sympathy because I experience the agony of being called upon myself and not knowing the answer. Again, this is *empathy*.

Vicarious experience and empathy are related in such a manner that they cannot be entirely separated. We think of the former as objective and the latter as subjective. In other words, vicarious experiences include the acquirement of knowledge gained by the acquaintanceship with the adventures of another, while empathy implies identification of yourself with another.

The value of vicarious experience is obvious. Suggested exercises for its development are:

Exercise VIII

1. Read a group of books that includes such types as the following:

    1. *Green Mansions* by W. H. Hudson.
    2. *Ethan Frome* by Edith Wharton.
    3. *David Copperfield* by Charles Dickens.
    4. *Vanity Fair* by William Makepeace Thackeray.
    5. *At the Bay* by Katherine Mansfield.
    6. *One More Spring* by Robert Nathan.
    7. *Man of Property* by John Galsworthy.

8. "The Almond Tree" by Walter de la Mare, in *The Riddle.*

9. *Jane Eyre* by Charlotte Brontë.

10. *Crime and Punishment* by Feodor Dostoevsky.

11. *Personal History* by Vincent Sheehan.

12. *Queen Victoria* by Lytton Strachey.

13. *Of Human Bondage* by Somerset Maugham.

14. *The Stars Look Down* by A. J. Cronin.

15. *Hunger* by Knut Hamsun.

16. *Wuthering Heights* by Emily Brontë.

17. *King of Elfland's Daughter* by Lord Dunsany.

2. See pictures including the works of such artists as Van Gogh, El Greco, Rembrandt.

3. Place yourself in the new surroundings suggested by the book or picture. Test the depth of your reactions by improvising a scene suggested to you by a character, a situation, or a mood, from the information you have received.

For example: in *Arrowsmith* there is a scene in which Arrowsmith is host at luncheon to two women. One is his fiancée, his engagement to whom he is anxious to break. The other is the girl whom he desires to marry. The student adapts the situation to himself in this manner: he is a young man in a similar dilemma. He enters a downtown restaurant with two imaginary characters from his own experience in a similar relationship to him. He talks to them and to the waiter with improvised lines, enacting the narrative outlined by the author.

For example: the student looks at Van Gogh's "Picture of a Young Man." He sees a handsome debonair youth with a zest for living and little comprehension of fear. He has the strength and warmth of sun-drenched soil. To one person he may mean the pioneer spirit of the early Californian; to another, the romance of a prince in the disguise of a peasant. He may even be associated with the abstraction of a summer holiday in the warm South, or the urbanity of the vagabond. Associations will differ with the individual according to his previous experience. Any narrative which has its inspiration from looking at this painting should be acted out according to the pattern devised by the student.

So far in connection with imagination the student has had exercises for "intensifying" emotion and for developing vision. Another consideration in the discussion of imagination is *fantasy*. We have already defined fantasy. When an actor is unable to connect directly with his past experience the elements of the picture he is conjuring he is employing *fantasy*. In other words, when the associations between the present picture and the actual experience are far-fetched to the degree that he cannot recognize them, he has employed *fantasy*.

For example: the actor is playing the role of the Man in the Moon in *The Princess Who Wouldn't Say Die*. The scene is in his house, which is made of green cheese. He is eating green turtle soup, when an arrow comes through the window and quivers in the wall.

The actor may find associations with actuality in his past experience such as green soup, the cooky house in *Hansel and Gretel,* and the sight of an arrow. But the actual appearance of the man, his distorted mannerisms, the exaggerated environment, the incongruity of an arrow and the moon, all these are considerably removed from his natural existence. It is apparent, then, that *fantasy* begins where actual *memory of experience* fades. It is well to keep in mind, however, that that experience is still serving a purpose, although unconsciously. Thus with minute analysis it would not be impossible to discover the components of the distorted mannerisms and the exaggerated environment.

In the theatre fantasy plays such an important part that considerable time should be devoted to it. It takes the form of whimsicality, mysticism, the dream play, and all the plays connected with the extravagant flight of imagination.

Take the following words, connect them in a story and act out the story in pantomime. The student is given ten minutes in which to plan the mode of action. The improvisation itself should take at least fifteen minutes. In this exercise the student's own character must be maintained. The association should be as far-fetched as possible.

For example: take the words *soap, door,* and *Christmas tree*. The student is walking on an enormous cake of wet soap trying to reach an enormous Christmas tree on which oranges the size of balloons are growing. He wants one of the oranges, but as he reaches for the nearest one a door closes, barring his approach. As he moves to another orange, the door again confronts him and closes in his face. He finally reaches an orange and gets it only after he has climbed to the top of the tree. He walks away from the tree, carrying the orange in front of him. He is about to take an enormous bite when he slips on the wet soap and falls.

Exercise IX

1. Sea ....violin ....pistol.
2. Cabin ....elevator ....streetcar.
3. Duchess ......plumber ....ski.
4. Ash tray ....electric bulb ....sea gull.
5. Aeroplane ....cup ....church steeple.
6. Window .....Africa ....cigarette.
7. Lollypop .....mermaid ....glove.
8. Candle ....deck of cards ....roof garden.
9. Sardine ......Bible ....davenport.
10. Comb ....wineglass ....magazine.
11. Necktie ......lampshade ....Mexico.
12. Nutcracker ...goldmine ....umbrella.
13. Rocking chair .cough drop ......zebra.
14. Pine tree .....pagoda ....balloon.
15. Ostrich ......bracelet ....raincoat.

Take the following words, connect them in a story, and act out the story with your own lines. This should be a group exercise. There should be allowed ten minutes in which the mode of action is planned by the group out of earshot of the rest of the class. Not more than three people should be used in a single problem. The improvisation itself should take about fifteen minutes. Again the characters of the students should remain unchanged, and the associations should be utterly strange.

Exercise X

1. Octopus ......angel ....shoe.
2. Daffodil .....window blind . . China.
3. Whale ....cartwheel ....tobacco leaf.

4. Carpet ...... dictionary .... clothes line.
5. Toothpick .... garden hose ...... theatre.
6. Garage .... mountain .... ocean liner.
7. Field mouse .. baseball bat ...... orange.
8. Orchid ...... bass violin .... aeroplane.
9. Radio .... lemon .... chimney.
10. Holiday ..... parsley .... dynamo.
11. Spectacles .... Norway .... red hair.
12. Garden ...... paintbrush .... surgery.
13. Party .... hyena .... Paris.
14. Boxing gloves milk bottle ...... palace.
15. Wig .... Australia .... ukelele.

Probably the most essential demand on the imagination is to believe in what the aural and visual imagination has created. This willingness to believe is most evident in a child at play.

For example: when the child plays school he becomes the teacher. His dolls or playmates become the pupils, and his surroundings become the schoolroom. He improvises without limitation. Time and space are no hindrance.

If the actor were as naïve in his acceptance of the playwright's pattern he would have little difficulty in simulating reality. Unfortunately, however, education and experience are designed to destroy illusion and to invite questioning. As the child grows older he ceases to accept his dream world as reality and is peremptory in his demands for facts. He even goes so far as to build safeguards of cynicism between himself and the unattainable.

It is of primary importance for the actor to break down this rebuttal of fancy and to restore to himself the capacity for accepting a given situation as truth. If he can attain the child's complete acceptance of the world he desires to surround him, he has found the way to establish reality for himself and for his audience.

How, then, does he go about recovering his naïveté? Such a recovery depends upon imagination and concentration. The part concentration plays we shall discuss in the next chapter. But imagination, with its components of intensification of emotion, visualization of aspects and transformation of environments, is the source from which it springs. In other words, "I believe because I imagine strongly." Therefore the more developed my ability to intensify feelings, the more reality those feelings have; the more developed my vision, the more reality the new physical aspects have. Naïveté will come, then, as the power of imagination increases. All the foregoing exercises are indirect approaches to its restoration.

In conclusion, let us repeat that the process of intensification of emotions, visualization, assimilation, and conviction is imagination. The more demands one makes on imagination, the more readily it will respond.

CHAPTER V

CONCENTRATION

In acting nothing must intrude between the actor and his task. No momentary diversion must disturb him from his business of doing and being what the author has intended for him. This ability to apply himself to the job at hand and to remain absorbed throughout its complete execution depends upon the development of what we call concentration.

In general, to concentrate is to focus sustained attention on one particular subject. It is true that while we are conscious we are always paying attention to something. When we are accused of being inattentive, or of not concentrating, we are merely giving our attention to the wrong thing. Thus one of the first problems in concentration is to direct attention to the *right point of interest.*

> *For example:* the right point of interest for the student is the teacher's lecture. We know that it is easy for the student's mind to wander from that lecture. In other words, his attention may be divided between the teacher and the things about him. To direct his attention he must select the teacher's lecture as his dominating interest to the exclusion of all else.

Well-directed attention, however, does not guarantee what we call complete concentration. There is the further problem of *sustaining* that attention.

> *For example:* the student may have little difficulty in listening to the opening words of the teacher's lectures but he may find his real problem in maintaining interest in that lecture throughout its duration.

If, then, the main problems of concentration are twofold —to *direct* attention and to *maintain* that attention—there must be methods to develop its proficiency. It stands to reason that the practice of good concentration in ordinary life will help to equip the actor for good concentration in the theatre. The part that concentration plays in the life of the actor is manifold:

1. To exhaust an experience which he may draw upon later, he must have learned to give his undivided attention to that experience.

2. To observe accurately the things he encounters about him, he must scrutinize them with undiverted inspection.

3. To intensify remembered emotion, to visualize a particular scene, and to convert artificial circumstances into reality, demand a mind riveted upon the task at hand.

Our first exercises will be devoted to the problem of directing attention. We know that there is little difficulty in directing attention to a subject which *interests* us.

> *For example:* we are easily absorbed in a conversation about ourselves. A discussion of the personal usually attracts us more easily than one of a more generalized nature.

It is well to note what some of the more interesting or more arresting subjects are. As stated above, the *personal* always adds importance to the discussion or appreciation of a subject. We know, too, that when there is an *emotional attachment* interest is more keen.

For example: in a heated argument, in a quarrel, or in circumstances of extreme amusement, attention is easily focused.

Increased knowledge also contributes to the allure of a subject.

For example: if we have a good background in stamp collecting and we are about to hear additional information on the topic, we are likely to be actively concerned. If, however, we know nothing of stamp collecting, we are apt to be bored.

On the other hand *curiosity* is a contributing factor.

For example: we are about to hear a lecture on a newly discovered planet. If that planet is in some way connected with our personal lives, or if knowledge of that planet supplements something we already know, or if the new discovery is an important topic of conversation, we are apt to display sharp curiosity concerning it.

We know, too, that the individual is more apt to respond to a subject when the *mind* and *body* of that individual are *alert.*

For example: we are told from psychological experiment that it is more satisfactory to study in a straight chair than in a too comfortable one. Again, it is easier to fix the attention of the well-rested mind than that of the fatigued one.

In summary, we find little difficulty in directing our attention to:

1. Subjects of personal interest.
2. Subjects with emotional attachment.
3. Subjects upon which we have increased knowledge.

4. Subjects about which we have a curiosity induced by our special background.

5. Subjects which we encounter when we are mentally and physically alert.

If our problem as actors, then, is to direct attention, it will be our duty to force one of the above qualifications on the material upon which we are supposed to focus attention. To endow a subject, which under ordinary circumstances might be dull and fail to attract us, with such a qualification, is to give that subject purpose.

> *For example:* we are to watch a travelogue on Norway. Scenery, let us say, has always been subordinate to people in our interests. We find ourselves glancing about the room instead of upon the screen before us. What purpose, then, is strong enough to attract us solely to the screen? If we call to mind the possibility of our playing Ibsen sometime in the future and of utilizing the information derived, we will have less difficulty in focusing our attention on the right place. Again, if we read a story of emotionally moving content before going to the travelogue—our interest will be stimulated. Any material on Norway, conversational or written, gathered before attending, will help. Furthermore, feeling especially fit and actively anticipating a new experience would aid us to select the right point of interest.

We may conclude that one method of focusing attention on a particular subject is to give yourself a positive purpose or reason for focusing that attention. Take the following exercises, and in doing them never lose sight of the fact that you are doing them for specific purposes. At the end of each exercise, teacher and student should discuss the difficulty or ease of concentration involved.

For example: one student is teaching another to play a game. He has fifteen minutes in which to teach the fundamentals. He desires his pupil to learn quickly and to give proof of his learning. Time and words are important. Neither student can afford to let attention or interest be diverted.

Exercise I

1. One student who knows the game of bridge teaches another who knows nothing of it some of the fundamentals. After twenty minutes of explanation, the student who is teaching questions the student being taught as to his assimilated knowledge.

2. One student who knows the game of hop-scotch teaches it to another, following the above procedure.

3. One student who knows puppetry teaches another to manipulate a stringed puppet.

4. One student who knows how to draw in perspective teaches another to draw a simple stage set in perspective.

5. One student tells another how to cook a favorite dish. The other student then repeats the instruction.

6. One student teaches another five colloquial foreign expressions to be used in ordering a dinner.

7. One student gives another exact directions to go to the depot. The student gives them back verbatim.

8. One student acting as stage manager gives directions to another student acting as assistant in regard to the setting of the stage. In the classroom with an improvised stage, the assistant carries out the directions.

9. One student explains to another how to start a car and how to put it in reverse. The second student does it in pantomime.

10. One student gives another information which should be included in a letter. He does not dictate it. The second student then incorporates the information in the letter which he writes.

The second group of exercises are done by the class as a whole.

For example: the teacher writes the names of ten cities in the United States on the board. The class is given a minute in which to center attention upon the list. At the end of the allotted time the list is erased, and the students write it from memory.

Exercise II

The teacher devises a list of:

1. Ten common terms such as box and automobile.
2. Ten nonsense syllables such as og, ort, and onk.
3. Ten automobiles.
4. Ten names of flowers.
5. Ten kinds of food.
6. Fifteen countries.
7. Fifteen proper names.
8. Fifteen letters of the alphabet.
9. Fifteen book titles.
10. Fifteen playwrights.

Exercise III

In this exercise the teacher should write the numbers on the board and give the students one minute to memorize them; then he erases the numbers, and the student reproduces as directed.

1. Given ten numbers of two figures each, as 89, 71.

2. Given five numbers of four figures as 3464, 8196.

3. Given five numbers of three figures as 317, 010.

4. Given three numbers, one of three figures and two of four, such as 998, 1776, and 1500. After the minute allotted for memorizing the figures, the students are directed to follow any given procedure, such as add the first and third and from the total subtract the second orally. This exercise should be repeated in various combinations.

5. Given a number of six figures as 685,165. The student after the allotted time for memorizing repeats the number backward; 685,165 should be done 561,586. This exercise should be repeated with two numbers of six figures each as the student progresses in facility.

In the following exercises, which are practically the same as those suggested under former headings, the student is given a limited amount of time in which to exhaust his material.

Exercise IV

1. The teacher brings to class several objects, such as a small wood carving or an etching. The students are given three minutes to examine the objects which the teacher keeps at the front of the room; the students are then given three minutes in which to describe the subject on which their attention has been centered.

This exercise should be repeated over a period of weeks until the teacher can be sure progress has been made in the development of complete application to the task at hand.

2. After three minutes of intent observation, one student gives a complete oral description of the other student with whom he is working. For this exercise, the entire class is divided into groups of two.

Exercise V

Simon says. This simple game is an excellent test of mental alertness and concentration. To play the game a leader must be selected. The duty of the leader is to call directions to the rest of the group, which they must follow instantly and accurately. Those directions are varied such as, Simon says, "Thumbs up"; Simon says, "Thumbs down"; Simon says, "Stand on one foot." The orders differ according to the imagination of the leader. When he fails to preface the command with the words "Simon says," the orders are not to be executed. Directions are given and executed rapidly. As soon as they miss, students are eliminated from the game. The game should be continued until all students are eliminated but one.

The foregoing exercises are intended to aid the student in learning to focus attention on one particular subject. Once he has learned to *direct* his attention to the right point of interest he has the further problem of *sustaining* that attention. We have learned that associating a *purpose* with a subject helps to attract us to that subject. If we *keep* the *achievement* of that purpose clearly in mind, we shall have little difficulty in *sustaining* interest.

For example: if we stop on the road to get directions to the nearest town, we listen intently until we have learned exactly what to do. Our *purpose* was to get the necessary information and only when the complete information is obtained have we achieved that *purpose.*

It follows, then, that keeping clearly in mind a strong purpose will not only assist us to direct attention but will enable us to sustain that attention. Furthermore, at all times the *accomplishment* of the purpose or task must be a motivating force.

For example: in listening to the travelogue on Norway, if we keep in mind that as actors the material is important, we must also realize that our job as listening actors is not over until every ounce of information has been obtained. The last two sentences may be even more important than the first two.

This carries into actual production of plays. Often it is said that a certain scene is dull material as far as the actor is concerned. It is probably one of obvious exposition. Such a scene is that between Christine and Nora in the first act of Ibsen's *The Doll's House.* If the actress playing Christine keeps in mind the fact that she has come to this household for the very important purpose of obtaining an opportunity to earn a livelihood, as well as to learn of the welfare of her friend, and if this purpose permeates her whole being, she cannot help but give color and interest to every question and answer throughout the long scene. On the other hand, if each interrogation and reply is a separate entity, not connected with an integrated motivating force, the scene becomes a dull, matter-of-fact routine of question and answer used only to explain the plot.

All that we have said so far about concentration points to the fact that it is a *positive* process. One does not improve concentration by weakening the interference, but by *strengthening* the point of interest. The shoemaker who is anxious to make a perfect pair of shoes gives himself whole-heartedly to the job. If, however, he is turning out simply one more of innumerable pairs of nondescript shoes, he is apt to be less attentive to his work. The actor who remembers why he, as a character, is upon the stage in a particular scene, will devote himself exclusively to the task. We know that often stage fright has been diminished not by negative suggestions as, "There is nothing to be afraid of—just relax," but by stressing the positive duty of the character. Let us take as an example the frightened beginner who must deliver a message to another character on the stage. The way he must help himself *positively* is to dwell on the fact that his present duty as a character, beyond all else in the world, is to deliver that message. Saying to himself, "I must imitate," or "I am concentrating," means the actor is concentrating not at all but is being diverted by the wish to concentrate. His purpose, then, is wrong, since it falls within the scope of his personality rather than within the scope of his character.

The following exercises vary from sheer mechanical exploits to short improvisations directly applied to acting. Some of the first ones may seem remote from acting but we must remember that any exercise which increases concentration in life increases concentration in the theatre.

Exercise VI

1. One half the class sing aloud a tune without words, while the other half whistle another tune softly to them-

selves. This exercise should be done until both groups can sustain their respective tunes to completion.

2. The class is divided into groups of two. One student must read a page silently, digesting all that is on that page, while simultaneously another student reads aloud from another book. The student who is reading silently must give the content of his page to the class when the exercise stops.

In the following group of exercises, students work together. They use their own characters but make up lines and stage business which apply to the situation as the scene develops. They are given three minutes before the scene starts to discuss the general scheme to be followed. They do not, however, make up lines and memorize them. This improvised scene should last not less than ten minutes and not more than twenty-five minutes. Attention should be directed not toward the excellence of the dialogue but toward the ability of each student to remain true to his purpose in the scene.

Exercise VII

1. Two girls are decorating the apartment in which they are to live. One girl is expecting visitors in a half hour and is anxious to have the apartment in order. The other girl resents the coming of the guests and attempts to prolong the work.

2. Four people are marooned on a desert island; each one wishes to follow his favorite method of government and living.

3. Two boys out of work who have not eaten for some time have the opportunity of robbing a third boy. The scruples of one boy are against it, while those of the second

boy are against starving. The outcome depends upon the outcome of the argument.

4. A young man tries to make an acquaintanceship with a young lady on a park bench. The girl is reluctant to talk without an introduction.

5. A young man catches the war spirit and feels it his duty to enlist. Two friends of his (girls or boys) try to dissuade him. The outcome depends upon the strongest arguments.

6. Three girls have been in an automobile accident, and one of them is critically ill in the hospital. The other two girls are now waiting in the hospital corridors for information concerning the condition of the third. They do everything possible to comfort one another and to learn news of their friend.

7. A young man returns home at six o'clock to break the news to his wife that he has lost his job. They have very little money and innumerable ambitions so that the ordeal of breaking the news is a very trying one.

8. Two girls left alone in a summer cottage are upstairs when they hear some one prowling about the house. They work out a plan of action and try to keep busy enough to alleviate their fears.

9. Three people who work together very harmoniously in an office are surprised by a representative from a national clothing corporation who brings news that one of them has won $25,000 in a slogan contest. The winner offers to take the others on a trip.

10. Two young actors who have not seen each other for three years meet in a restaurant. Each is afraid to tell the other of the fact that he or she has a job in a new show

for fear of discouraging the other who is out of work. Their conversation finally reveals that they have both been hired in the same cast of a new show.

In regard to the importance of positive methods of concentration, experienced actors work out many individual devices. Often one actor uses a way of clearing his mind which seems wholly contradictory to that of another actor. Some actors are silent for a period of time before entering, talking to no one about them in the wings. Others will talk on irrelevant subjects until the moment for stepping on to the stage. Whatever works to enable the individual to enter the stage in character and to keep clearly before him the reasons for his character's presence in the scene will be right for that particular actor. We are inclined to believe that the one in which the actor is silent for a time before entrance is more satisfactory than most methods. That silence must be one in which he is doing positive constructive thinking. He must feel and think the things which would anticipate the character's entrance into the scene. This helps to clarify for him the place and happenings from which he is coming and prepares him for the environment to which he is going.

The actor is apt to think that by silently saying to himself, "I am now walking up the steps, I am feeling sad, I hate to enter the room," he is concentrating on the right material before his entrance. This is not true, however, for again he is being diverted by the wish to concentrate.

For example: Eilert Lovborg, as he waits in the hall in Ibsen's *Hedda Gabler* should be experiencing mingled feelings of curiosity and excitement. He does this not by saying, "How excited I am!", or "How curious I am!", but by wondering what Hedda's point of view will be, how she will greet him, what Tesman will say to his book, and by recalling Hedda's former power to fascinate him. He may do this by giving himself positive silent lines, but these lines must be as true and absorbing as any lines he speaks on the stage. They must be filled with emotion and thought, but must in no sense be abstract comments such as, "How curious am I!" They should be lines which follow a thought pattern just as consistently as good dialogue does. Good dialogue on the stage does not differ night from night. In the same way this well worked out thought pattern should remain constant. For instance, as Lovborg watches the maid go in to announce his presence, the following thoughts might flash across his mind: "Have I the manuscript with me?" He feels for it and finds it in his pocket. He hears voices in the living-room—"That's Tesman's voice and Hedda's. I wonder who else is talking. Can Hedda be as thrilling as ever?" With this thought should come attraction for Hedda, and next the desire to leave the house at once. "If I could only leave now! But why should I? Tesman himself sent for me." The maid returns, nods to Eilert to enter. He murmurs "Thanks" to her and walks into the room. Simultaneously he realizes the presence of Hedda, Tesman, and a third person, whom he identifies as Judge Brack. His eyes rest, however, on Tesman and he says the line "Thanks for your letter, Tesman."

These silent lines which are so important in helping to prepare the actor for an entrance are equally important on the stage. When there are more than two characters on the stage and one remains silent for a period of time, he sometimes finds his attention wandering while awaiting his cue.

To prevent this lapse of interest, he must give himself a positive function in the scene. As in life when he listens to two other people talking he mentally digests and comments upon the material he overhears, so on the stage he must go through the same process. If he is deliberately ignoring the conversation, that process, too, should be positive. He must think the thoughts which enable him to disregard the others. It will be easier for him to guarantee his attention in this particular scene, if he works out a suitable thought pattern of definite reactions which he undergoes as religiously as he adheres to the written dialogue the author has given him.

This supplying of silent lines, pictures, thoughts, or fragmentary lines and thoughts, often occurs in dialogue between only two people, even where there is no pause indicated.

For example: two people on a darkened stage which represents a street at night, look up at a lighted window, behind which a dinner table can be seen. The author gives the following lines:

A. That room looks so cozy.

B. It would be nice to be in France now.

The lines seem to be unrelated unless one can follow the thought pattern of "B." Looking at a lighted window reminded him of the most effectively lighted windows he had ever seen. These were on a ship passing the one on which he was making the crossing to Europe. The idea of Europe was associated with his favorite country, France, and brought with it a nostalgia which motivated him to say the seemingly unrelated line, "It would be nice to be in France now."

In this case, the actor did not formulate lines in his head such as, "I remember the ship I saw," but he allowed the *picture* of the ship to flash through his mind. Another example in which an actual line might be formulated is:

A. You can't leave the house today.

B. Anything you say.

Actually, before "B" says, "Anything you say," there flashes through his mind the following line and its accompanying feeling:

B. I hate you—you spoiled everything I wanted to do—but I don't dare risk your anger; I'd better smile and shut up.

All we hear aloud, then, is "Anything you say."

If the actor keeps himself occupied throughout a performance with ideas as positive as these we have suggested, he will have little time or inclination to be diverted, and concentration will be guaranteed.

The following exercises will give the student practice in the application of the foregoing suggestions. The students are to maintain their own characters throughout. Only the situation is fictitious.

Exercise VIII

1. A young man or woman is about to enter an employment office. The student should do his thinking out loud. The exercise ends when the student enters the door.

2. A young man or woman returns home after having run away five years earlier. As he walks up to the house and stops a moment before entering, we hear his thoughts aloud.

3. A young man is going to enter the house of a young lady to whom he is about to propose.

4. A young man or woman is about to enter the sick-room of his or her mother, where he or she has to hide the fact that the condition of the mother is critical.

5. A young man or woman is about to enter the stage where diplomas and awards are to be distributed at graduation. He or she knows he has won the highest award.

6. Repeat the improvisations found in Exercise VII. Add a person who remains quiet during the scene, but who is part of that scene. Let the student recall, as nearly as possible, his line of thought and repeat it to the class at the end of the exercise.

7. Let two students take the following lines and create and demonstrate circumstances and thought patterns which might connect the thought.

A. I wonder what kind of a man Dillinger was.
B. I saw *The Petrified Forest* last night.
A. It would be interesting to serve on a jury.

8. Following the above directions the students are given the following lines.

A. Ivy grows all along the wall in our back yard.
B. There's the most beautiful spaniel next door.
A. One shouldn't be too neighborly.

9. A. Listen to that train whistle.
B. Leather goods are very expensive.
A. Boat travel is so much cleaner.

10. A. I have a bad headache.
B. Have you read *Consumer's Research* lately?
A. We surely need socialized medicine.

CHAPTER VI

CHARACTERIZATION

WHEN the actor is able to realize a prescribed role as the author has conceived it, and when he is able to enact that role so that the audience believes in its reality and individuality, *then* and *only then* can he be said to have a *characterization.*

To give character to a role means to endow that role with the mental faculties, the emotions, the peculiarities of personality, the physical aspect, and the personal mannerisms which are the integral part of a particular human being. The actor will find that this particular person conceived by the author is a new individual, who, though he may have many familiar traits, displays those traits in a proportion and degree different from any other individual.

For example: on first examination of the part of Hamlet, an actor discovers certain general characteristics. These obvious attributes are Hamlet's youth, his supersensitivity, his extraordinary intelligence, his royal background, his morbid frame of mind and his consciousness of the intrigue about him. As the actor develops his character he will find he has incorporated some of these attributes in former characterizations. Perhaps he played the Student Prince at one time, a character of similar age and background. Perhaps he played Peter Standish in *Berkeley*

Square, a character of like sensitivity and introspection. In this way we might find similarities to any number of other roles. In the particular case of Hamlet these qualities appear in a new combination. While Hamlet has youth and the royal blood of the Student Prince, and the sensitivity and introspection of Peter Standish, he also has many additional characteristics which are peculiar to Hamlet alone. In other words while one or two of the ingredients are found in others the complete combination is never duplicated.

Not only will the combination be different but the degree of intensity in which he possesses these attributes will vary. Both Hamlet and Peter Standish are intelligent, but Hamlet's intelligence appears to be keener and more developed. Both Hamlet and the Student Prince have royal backgrounds, but while the Student Prince finds in his family connections mild discomfiture, Hamlet finds tragedy and death. In conclusion, although the three characters possess many of the same qualities, those qualities differ in proportion, in degree, and in circumstance. One might easily compare the elements in a new characterization to the cards in a hand of bridge, for while the cards are the same, each hand differs with every new deal.

In connection with the creation of character an actor has two problems. One is to discover wherein the person he is attempting to bring to life is similar to himself and others, and different from himself and others. The second is to assimilate all this material and mold it into a plausible reality within the boundaries of the play. Characterization, then, is a matter of analysis and synthesis.

How then does the actor set about this first task of finding similarities and differences between the individual he is attempting to create and all other persons?

To begin with, he uses for a basis of comparison his own emotions and experiences, observation of himself and others, and the full scope of his imagination. Much of this he has already learned to do from former exercises. In order that the student may grasp the simplest fundamentals of a characterization, it is well to begin with improvisations suggested by the teacher, rather than with written roles from a play. To some extent this has been included in previous exercises, for it is true that in portraying the simplest problem in observation we have taken our first steps in characterization. As we watched a clerk behind a counter, we noted what she did or did not do which differentiated her from any one else.

For example: the actor is given the problem of improvising the character of a young man of impoverished circumstances who is going blind, and who decides to commit suicide. Here is a comparatively simple problem, since no actual lines, relationships, nor circumstances limit the student. He works out his own thoughts, emotions, and behavior, using for his guidance the above outline.

His first effort is to search his own experience for emotions of fear, suffering, pain, worry, and any other accompanying feelings. Through definite comparison with incidents in his own life or incidents he has observed in the lives about him, and through the magnification by imagination of the feelings thus derived he creates the *emotions* peculiar to his character. After he has reconstructed the emotional reactions of his character he must work out what we call a careful *thought pattern.* A thought pattern is an outline of thinking which is arrived at by an analysis of the mind of the character and the reactions this character has to incumbent circumstances. Now with the perception of his character, his youth, physical privation, and anguish, and with the thought pattern which is in this case one leading to decisive action, he sets about his procedure as planned or as the scene suggests. Through concentration he should be able to maintain an uninterrupted stream of thought and sensation. Suppose he comes to the conclusion that taking a poison is the easiest method. He visualizes the room, experiences the emotions, thinks the corresponding thoughts and undergoes the action attendant upon the decision he has made. The action in this case may be going to a cupboard, fumbling for the right medicine, seating himself, and drinking the potion. Of course his actions will be tempered by the period, the costume, and the physical environment of the era against which his character is played.

The following exercises are to assist the student in understanding the demands of his character. A character is given to the student, who returns to class the next day prepared to describe aloud what thoughts, feelings and behavior would distinguish the individual from all other persons. He arrives at his conclusions by experimentation at home and by careful analysis. He is not asked to act this character in class, but merely to explain it.

Exercise I

1. An earnest young person who has been working for five years at routine office work invents a new kind of pencil sharpener which is destined for success.
2. A sophisticated young person recently graduated from

a large university arrives to accept a teaching position in a small country town where the standards of living are crude and uncomfortable.

3. A tired clerk in a department store is called to the manager's office to describe a bill of goods which he or she has just sold to a thief using a fictitious account.

4. An indignant landlady goes through the belongings of a roomer who has failed to pay rent and finds a valuable diamond ring.

5. A boastful automobile salesman who is demonstrating a car to a prospective buyer discovers it will not start.

6. A professional card-sharp organizes a game of bridge on a boat and is apprehended by the captain.

7. A famous moving picture star discovers there will be no renewal of her contract. She threatens to sue the producer.

8. An unmanageable boy of high-school age takes the blame for breaking a window to save a younger brother.

9. A successful artist discovers that a mural for a public building will not be accepted on account of its political suggestion.

10. A woman of social prominence, having planned a reception for foreign notables, receives at the eleventh hour a telegram informing her of their inability to attend.

11. A picket in front of a restaurant is falsely accused by the police of breaking a near-by window.

12. A doctor's wife who has planned a summer vacation with her husband is called upon to give it up because of an impending operation her husband must perform.

13. A soldier who has lost an arm is decorated for unusual bravery under fire. He is in the hospital at the time he receives the honor.

14. A famous ballerina who pretended to be a Russian exile is discovered to be May Smith of Brooklyn.

15. A tropical explorer in the midst of a speech at a women's club is interrupted by a woman in the audience who accuses him of bigamy.

The next exercises are designed to teach the student to enact the similarities and differences in the character. By recollection of emotion the student should relate every feeling and thought to actual experience. In the first ten exercises this should be done aloud. In the second ten the student may undergo the process of recollection silently. Only the enactment will be seen by the class and teacher. Now class criticism should be encouraged for the purpose of discussion and clarification.

For example: the student who is to improvise the young man about to go blind is given ten minutes to outline in his mind the general behavior of his character. He decides he will begin by entering the door of his small living quarters after having received a doctor's verdict. What his exact movements in the room will be, he leaves to the inspiration of the moment. The sources of this inspiration may be many—perhaps a window, a bureau, or anything of the sort. In this case the sight of an imagined cupboard may suggest the poison. Some of these actions he will think of before he starts the improvisation, but others will come to him as he works. He knows that his emotions will be first despair, then bitterness, then self-pity, and finally a resentment against his fate strong enough to drive him to suicide. For each of these emotions he repeats aloud an experience of his own, either actual or vicarious. He recalls his behavior during those earlier experiences and may incorporate some of it as part of the action in the scene. Thus he has drawn on observation as well as on memory of emotion. Many of these experiences are inadequate and he finds they will have to be intensified by imagination. This should not be difficult if his imagination has been developed by constant exercise and training.

Now the student goes through the actual business connected with the completion of the scene. When the exercise is completed the class and teacher should base their criticism on the following questions:

1. Has the actor established the age of the character?
2. Is the action he goes through clear and plausible?
3. Is the action related to the size and contents of the room?
4. Are the emotions genuine?
5. Do the actions flow out of a careful thought pattern?
6. What behavior distinguished this person from all other persons?
7. Can the onlookers differentiate between the appearance and behavior of the character they have just seen and that of the student who enacted it?

The first problems should be done in pantomime. This does not mean that because no lines are spoken orally thought patterns are unnecessary. The process of thinking should be orderly and definite so that the actions or stage business will be motivated properly.

Exercise II

1. A girl of eighteen, reared in an orphan asylum and now working in a factory, is summoned to appear at the bedside of a dying woman. This woman, she has been told,

is her sister, who has known of the girl's struggles, but fearing that recognition would endanger her social prestige, has allowed her to remain in the orphan asylum. The girl enters the room prepared to hate the woman lying on the hospital bed, and discovers that she is dead. She walks to the dresser and examines the picture of the woman's husband, and in examining it begins to understand why her sister kept silent so long. She returns to the bed, covers the face, and exits.

2. An impressionable girl of sixteen, finishing her last year of high school and anticipating all that college will hold, has been practicing for an hour. It is a grey day, the middle of January. She is sitting at the piano playing without spirit. Finally she breaks off, and walks over to the window. She looks out, wishing for something to happen. At that moment a heavy truck swings into the street and hits a small boy who has been playing there.

3. A New York girl, reared in comfortable surroundings, has been left penniless. She has had no specialized training. During the economic crisis she has been forced to look for work. The best thing available is a small primary school in Kansas. We see her entering the dilapidated farm house in which she is to reside during her school year. The room is a combination kitchen and living-room. The table is covered with unappetizing food, the smells are not of the choicest, and the sink is filled with dirty dishes. A work-ridden woman stands and eyes her from the sink. Unkempt children seem to be peering from all corners. She is horrified, but tries to conceal her distaste and make a friendly approach to the woman. The door was answered by a large brutish man. She greets him first, and then the woman.

4. A girl, twenty-five years of age, has been ill for two years. She has been in a sanitorium all this time. Her doctors have assured her that she will recover, but she knows without being told that her days are numbered. Today is one of the first beautiful days of spring. For the first time in two years she will be allowed to open the French windows of her room, which is on the ground floor, and walk out into the garden. As she walks down the garden path from flower to flower, her happiness is mingled with regret and perhaps a little self-pity. An aeroplane passes above her. A bird flies by. The sun goes behind a cloud and suddenly the air becomes chill. She returns to her room hurriedly.

5. A thief who is not a professional, but is forced by hunger to plunder, enters a second story bedroom and examines the room. The room is one in a home of considerable magnificence. He becomes so absorbed in the objects in it that he fails to hear approaching footsteps. He is amazed to hear the door open and to be confronted by a very frightened young lady.

6. A lawyer reopens a house in which he and his divorced wife lived. He examines the living-room and finds letters which recall the early days of his marriage.

7. A very bashful boy waits on the stage to be called upon to give the valedictory address for his graduating class. He waits for his turn and finally walks to the speakers' stand for the address.

8. A worker without a job goes back to explain the predicament of himself and his fellow workers to his former employer. On entering the office he finds the employer to be a friend of his youth. He shows in his general bearing the contempt he feels for the employer and his point of view.

9. An unemployed man stands on the dock watching the employees of a produce company destroy a cargo of bananas by throwing it from the boat into the harbor. The owners are anxious to create a higher market price.

10. A spinster school teacher welcomes spring by attending a band concert in a park. While enjoying the music a young couple sitting beside her remark on her peculiarity. She realizes that they are talking about her. Her day spoiled, she rises and goes home.

The following exercises are done in pantomime, although the student concludes the exercise with one spoken word. All additional people in these exercises exist only in pantomime.

Exercise III

1. A girl arrives at the home of a woman to whom she is to apply for a position of social secretary. She is shown in by a butler and waits in the living-room for the lady of the house. After a few moments the woman enters and the girl says, "How do you do?"

2. A young man arrives at the studio of a Viennese singing teacher. He is realizing a lifelong ambition. The wife of the teacher admits him to the studio and leaves him to wait for the teacher. As the boy waits, he nervously examines the room. The singing teacher arrives. His appearance is a shock to the boy. He attempts to hide his surprise.

3. A young actor expects a telephone call from a producer. He keeps himself busy so that his mind will not wander to the telephone. Finally the bell rings and he composes himself sufficiently to answer in a normal tone.

4. A disappointed young man in college has quarreled

with his girl. He goes to his room and disconsolately starts packing. The telephone rings. It is the girl, who has called to apologize.

5. A mother of a family of five is cleaning up the debris after a picnic at Coney Island. There is sand in everything. The weather is very hot and she is exhausted. Her husband returns and suggests another picnic the following Sunday. She answers with one sentence.

6. A successful actress goes to an art exhibit in Paris and sees a picture she admires. The curator, watching her admiration, approaches her and tells her the name of the artist. She is amazed to find that it is a young man whom she loves. She praises the picture to the curator.

7. A chemist has been experimenting in a laboratory and completes an experiment he has been working on for some time. He telephones the professor in charge.

8. A prisoner who has refused to speak to visitors or guards is passing the time in his cell. His mother is brought to the cell door and he makes the first remark he has made since he was brought there two weeks before.

9. A worker of indefinite political leanings watches a May Day parade, and catching sight of his fellow workers marching, is inspired to join them. He calls to them as he approaches their ranks.

10. A young person is writing a letter preparatory to leaving home. As the envelope is being sealed the mother enters the room and inquires as to the contents of the letter. The answer is given briefly.

The next exercises include both action and the necessary words. All properties and other characters are still imaginary.

Exercise IV

1. A young man before a magistrate refuses to go to war.

2. An old lady sells apples to an after-theatre crowd in a New York street. She converses with customers as they pass.

3. A shop girl, accused of stealing, testifies on the witness stand.

4. A middle-class American tourist shops in a linen store in Florence, Italy.

5. A tired mother of four children, living in a tenement, explains to the owner why she cannot pay the rent.

6. A girl in a ticket booth of a moving picture house talks to the ticket buyers, some of whom she knows.

7. A conceited writer of nominal success orders luncheon in a fashionable restaurant.

8. An elderly employee in a furniture store is called into the manager's office and dismissed.

9. An old woman in an old people's home tells her story. It is a lie.

10. A prominent stock broker is in conference when he is called to the telephone. He is called by the chief of police, who informs him that his son has been arrested on charges of swindling.

In the chapter on observation the question arose as to whether personal mannerisms observed in others for use in characterization might not lead to imitation. We made the point that if these mannerisms or qualities are recorded without an understanding of their motivation, they will remain imitations or superimposed attributes. We repeat here that no reproduction, no matter how accurate, may be called a re-creation until it is the direct expression of the inner consciousness.

The following exercises are suggested to enable the student to incorporate the material observed into the integral part of the character he is attempting to create. In these exercises the student first demonstrates the particular action or quality observed, then he explains why such an action occurred. Next, he re-creates the character, attempting to incorporate the qualities of mind, body, and emotion which resulted in the particular action.

For example: in watching the teacher the student may have noticed that he continuously runs his fingers slowly through his hair from his forehead to the base of his skull. It is not enough to repeat this action in the role of the teacher we may be playing. We must find what sequence of thoughts and feelings gave rise to the action. These we must experience as our very own in order to substantiate our own action. In this case, the student learns that the particular person whom he is examining is a slow thinker and has conditioned himself to begin a thought as he touches his forehead and complete it as the hand leaves the base of his neck.

It is more important that the student learn to re-create this individual's rhythm of thinking than that he reproduce the gesture. If now, through constant practice, he can catch this thinking process and can attach this gesture as a natural accompaniment, he may keep it in his characterization. If not, the gesture will remain a meaningless superficiality.

The following topics, which have already been used in

observation, are suggested again at this point. This time, however, the actions observed should be related directly to their source in the mental and emotional make-up of the character. As a result the characterization should be more complete. They may or may not include words. They should be taken directly from life. Certain qualifications such as age have been added for a further problem.

Exercise V

1. Watch a doctor between twenty and thirty years of age.
2. Watch a doctor between sixty and seventy years of age.
3. Watch a lawyer with a promising career.
4. Watch a clerk who is comparatively new at the job.
5. Watch a floor walker who is very efficient.
6. Watch a waiter who enjoys his work.
7. Watch a mechanic who knows his craft.
8. Watch a factory worker who dislikes his job.
9. Watch a streetcar conductor who is tired.
10. Watch a student who is attempting to be an artist.
11. Watch a newsboy who receives a first edition of the evening paper.
12. Watch a typist between twenty and thirty years of age.
13. Watch a typist between forty and fifty years of age.
14. Watch a peddler selling a trick toy device on the street.
15. Watch a salesman sell shoes in the morning.
16. Watch the same salesman sell shoes late in the afternoon.
17. Watch a dance orchestra leader.
18. Watch a torch singer who has been on the job for many years.

19. Watch a picket who believes in the effectiveness of what he is doing.

20. Watch a hairdresser.

As the character's actions, feelings, and thoughts grow stronger, the actor's own personal characteristics and preoccupations give way to their dominance. When his own personality is satisfactorily subordinated to that of the new individual he has created, then he may be said to have a characterization. Unless his emotions are genuine, his thoughts definite and true to his character, his actions clearly motivated, unless his concentration is sustained, his character will remain superficial.

When the actor understands what the character's essential qualities are, he is ready to assimilate them. Merely knowing what they are does not constitute a characterization. The actor must first perceive them. This is what we mean when we say the actor "feels" the part. Then when the part is perceived, it comes to life through the absorption of the actor into it. In other words, the actor does not assimilate the character but is assimilated into it. The steps to realization of a character are understanding, perception, and assimilation.

So far this chapter has been devoted to methods for understanding the character. Exercises and discussions found elsewhere in this book should enable an actor to arrive at a state where perception is comparatively easy. Perception will occur to him when his body is free, his understanding clear, his attention concentrated entirely upon the life he is portraying, and his belief complete in the reality of what he is doing.

Assimilation is the state which occurs when the actor's perception is so keen that his own stream of consciousness gives way to the stream of consciousness of his character. He does not lose his own mind and feeling, but finds them entirely subordinated to those of his character. In other words, for the time being the actor becomes the character and yet retains his own consciousness.

If the actor has successfully mastered the exercises in this book he has achieved a certain amount of facility in assuming a character. From now on his development depends upon application of these principles to definite problems in characterization. He is ready now to work on more complex characters in more complex situations. These must include both exercises in improvisation and characterization from scripts.

The degree of ease with which an actor is able to grasp the stream of consciousness of the character is the measure of his talent. This predilection for the assumption of another's inner life may be called a talent for acting.

CHAPTER VII

THE ACTOR'S MEDIUM

In the field of creative work oftentimes the artist has the advantage of an instrument which in itself has beauty and value. The tones of the violin are an advantage to the musician, the color of his paints is an advantage to a painter. The actor, on the other hand, has no objective tools, and as a result has the added responsibility of being both creator and the instrument from which the creation materializes.

The actor's body is his medium of expression. If this is true what physical qualifications should that body possess?

It is to the actor's benefit to be built in good average proportions, but many fine actors have had no such good fortune. Some, even, have had physical handicaps. Whether his body is beautiful is not the deciding factor in the success of an actor. The primary requisite of the actor's body is pliability rather than beauty. His muscles should be developed and mobile. His movements must be co-ordinated and easy. His gestures must flow freely and naturally. He must develop the capacity to relax so that his entire body will be liberated enough to respond quickly and easily to the need of any possible action.

The actor's physical training should start from the time he is a small child. It should consist of gymnastics, games of physical exertion, eurythmics, and dancing. The child's body is plastic and for the actor it is of primary importance that this plasticity be preserved. It is during the years of adolescence that this freedom is endangered. Preoccupation with academic life, the necessity to earn a living, self-consciousness of the growing body, and other factors tend to lessen physical activity and to allow inhibitions to develop in early youth. If the aspiring actor can be made conscious of the need for organized exercise during the years between eleven and eighteen he will be saved much grief later in his career. In the average dramatic school, however, students enter after this formative stage. Many bad habits have been acquired, and many needs neglected. It is this situation for which we must prescribe.

From the day the teacher of acting encounters the student he must insist that his physical training begin. There is neither time nor facility to do adequate body training in the acting class. This work must be done in the gymnasium, the playfield, the eurythmics class, and the dance studio. The actor should be doing this work for at least one to two hours a day. In the college, opportunities for such study are many, and it is the duty of the acting teacher to insist that his students participate in them. In the high school there are similar advantages. In the community theatre there are always available gymnastic and dancing teachers who are willing to co-operate.

Of course some time in the acting class will be devoted to walking, sitting, moving, and gesturing, but the teacher of acting can only describe the form, beauty, and nature of those movements. The instructor has little time to train the students in the actual muscular control.

Too much emphasis cannot be placed on the importance of body training. All phases of the modern dance should be studied at one time or another. Ballet will contribute form and co-ordination. Interpretive dancing will contribute methods of freedom and relaxation. Certain schools of the dance emphasize effective relations of body to space. Others will be important for character and pantomime. All of them will teach centralization of power, utilization of space, balance, and grace.

Where there are teachers of eurythmics available these classes are very valuable. They develop flexibility, the sense of rhythm, and absolute co-ordination between mind and body. Fencing, too, is a necessary attribute for the actor, for it develops relaxation, poise, and concentration.

The teacher of acting can do a great deal for the student in regard to relaxation. In the method which we have described for enabling the student to be absorbed in the *purpose* for his presence on the stage we find one mode of release. The actor is so immersed in the task at hand that there is no time for such a question as "What shall I do with my hands?" The hands have their job as well as the voice. It is nervousness which stiffens the actor and it is self-consciousness which is responsible for nervousness. If then the teacher or director can show the student how to subordinate self to the demands of the particular situation in the play he will teach him to relax.

A question which is often brought up in the classroom in regard to relaxation is "If my character is tense and nervous, shouldn't I be tense and nervous?" The answer is that there is a difference between the tenseness of the character and the tenseness of the actor portraying that character. The specific difference is that the actor can turn this nervousness on and off at will. When he must relax for the purpose of rest he will be able to do so quickly and easily. He can also resume the tenseness of the character at the proper time. Young actors err in losing control and allowing the state of tenseness to *dominate them*.

This question of control also enters into the problem of mannerisms. It may be said of the young actress attempting to play Sadie Thompson in *Rain* that her slouching posture is just right for the part. This is a disadvantage rather than an advantage to the actress attempting to play the role. There are moments in the play when Sadie Thompson will want to break this mannerism of standing and change to another. If that posture is a personal characteristic of the actress she will find it difficult to change at will. It will involve all the trouble of breaking a habit. The point is that the actor must be free from his own personal mannerisms in order to express adequately and easily the mannerisms of his character; otherwise he has the tendency to superimpose himself upon his character rather than to subordinate himself to the demands of the individual he is portraying. The actor remains a creative artist so long as he is in control of his medium.

It is the duty of the actor to himself and to the theatre to keep physically fit. His health is his investment. There is no more demanding work in the world than acting. It calls for an alert mind and a sound body. These are to be found only where regular habits and intelligent precaution are practiced to combat illness.

We suggest certain definite exercises which will help to free and to relax the students before classroom work and before rehearsal. These must not substitute for all physical activity suggested in this chapter. They are merely a minor aid.

Exercise I

Position: Stand with the feet astride, knees straight.

Exercise: Bend forward, relaxing the torso, arms, and neck. Bounce the torso up and down rhythmically, loosening all but the leg muscles.

Exercise II

Position: Lie on the back, arms at the sides, legs straight.

Exercise: Tighten all the body muscles. Inhale. Relax and exhale.

Exercise III

Position: Sit on the floor, knees bent. Grasp the ankles with the hands. The ankles are held throughout the exercise.

Exercise: Roll backwards on a curved back, straightening the legs up into the air. Roll forward, bending the knees as you roll. Finish by sliding the heels along the floor until the legs are straight. Repeat.

Exercise IV

Position: Lie on the back, knees pulled up against the chest. Push the legs into the air, at the same time elevating the hips. Brace the hips in this position with the hands, elbows on the floor.

Exercise: Move the legs in the air as if pedaling a bicycle.

Exercise V

Position: Standing.

Exercise: On count *one* swing the right foot in front of

the left, at the same time swinging the left arm forward and the right arm back. Count *two,* swing the right foot in back of the left, at the same time bringing the left arm back and the right arm forward. Count *three,* swing the right foot forward, right arm back and left arm forward. Repeat, beginning with the alternate foot. This exercise should be one of relaxed, flowing movement.

Exercise VI

Position: Lie on the back, arms at the sides, palms down, legs straight.

Exercise: Keeping the knees straight and the toes pointed, kick the legs into the air alternately, without touching the heels to the floor.

Exercise VII

Position: Right toe pointed to the right, right hand on the hip, left arm curved over the head. Lean the torso and head to the right.

Exercise: Push the hip with the right hand, leaning the torso to the right on the counts *one, two, three, four.* On count *four* bring the torso back to the erect position. Repeat, alternating sides.

Exercise VIII

Position: Feet astride, clasp the left hand with the right against the right shoulder, torso twisted to the right.

Exercise: Bring the hands across the body down to the left foot as if chopping wood. The movement should be vigorous. Repeat, using alternate sides.

Exercise IX

Position: Stand with the feet comfortably astride. Raise the arms even with the shoulder, elbows bent, hands in front of the chest. The forearms and hands should be relaxed.

Exercise: On count *one* jerk the elbows back as far as they will go, keeping the forearms and hands still relaxed. On count *two* fling the arms into the air vigorously. Repeat.

Exercise X

Position: Lie on the stomach, arms extended over the head, legs together. Relax.

Exercise: Arching the back, pull arms, legs, and head up from the floor as far as possible. Relax and repeat.

Exercise XI

Position: Stand bent forward from the hips with the arms and neck relaxed.

Exercise: Swing the torso from side to side, using an even rhythm.

Exercise XII

Position: Sit on the floor, legs extended in front, knees straight, feet apart.

Exercise: Bend torso as near to the floor as possible on a count of *one, two, three, four*. On count *four* return to the first position. Repeat.

Exercise XIII

Position: Standing. Arms at sides.

Exercise: On count *one* jump to a wide stride position.

At the same time clap the hands high over the head. On count *two* return to the first position. Repeat.

Exercise XIV

Position: Standing. Hands on hips.

Exercise: Rotate the trunk in a complete circle, using four counts. Count *one,* torso forward; count *two,* to the left; count *three,* back; count *four,* to the right. Repeat.

CHAPTER VIII

VOICE AND SPEECH

If there is one lesson to be learned from the actors of the old school, it is the importance of a rich voice and clear diction. It is the tendency of modern actors in their efforts for "naturalism" to slight projection and to be satisfied with slovenly enunciation. The beginning actor should be made to realize that tone and speech are the two most essential tools with which he works. They must be developed with relentless study and care. Of the actor's medium, they are the most ostentatious attributes, and consequently the ones by which he is most often judged.

The development of tone production is one thing; the cultivation of diction, another. Both are closely related, but both are important enough to receive separate emphasis and study.

Work in tone production is concerned with correcting faults in breathing, and faults in pharyngeal and laryngeal responses. In regard to breathing, the most common faults are first, lack of rhythm due to nervousness, to timidity, to superficial reading or thinking, or to insufficient self-confidence. There are various remedies for this. Among them are rest, work on selections of vital interest or conviction, more careful analysis and study of the material to be interpreted, and for cases of extreme nervousness, consultation with the physician or psychologist. A second breathing fault is weak and sluggish inhalation. Causes for this may be fatigue, poor health, laziness, or slouch habits. Suggested remedies are rest and gymnastics, and work on excerpts from plays or any other reading material which is particularly exciting. A third defect is mouth breathing. Causes for this may be adenoids or some other physical constriction, habit, or lack of confidence. Suggestions for correction are vocal exercises which have been designed to establish relaxation and co-ordination, consultation with a physician, exercises for improving general conditions of health, and advice from the teacher for developing confidence. Audible breathing is also a handicap for the actor. It may be due to constrictions in the summit of the pharynx, or in the pillars of the soft palate, to abnormal obstructions in the air passages or to too concentrated nose or mouth breathing. Help for it is medical examination, and oral work to establish co-ordination which will result in relaxation of the throat. There is, too, the danger of breathing too seldom. This happens when impressions are not deep enough and reading is too hurried and superficial. Tenseness due to inability for relaxation may be the root of this evil. It may be remedied by the development of concentration, the establishment of the conditions for relaxation, and more deliberate individualization of ideas through oral reading. The reading of reposeful, dignified selections has been found helpful for this defect. Still another fault is collar-bone breathing. Its causes may be timidity, an hysterical attitude of mind, bad instruction, or self-consciousness. An understanding of the breathing process may be the cure for this. Among other exercises the reading of passages of a slow, rhythmic nature is helpful. Labored breathing due to bad instruction or the forcing of the center of breathing too low, is another danger. Its remedies are the same as those for collar-bone breathing. In short, good breathing means taking in an adequate supply of air through unobstructed passages, resulting in a sympathetic, elastic fullness or activity in the middle of the body in the region of the diaphragm, and a simultaneous passivity and opening of the throat or tone passage.

Pharyngeal faults are first, throatiness due to tight jaw, constriction in the neighborhood of the back of the tongue and lower pharynx, and lack of centralized breathing. Remedies are systematic exercises in breathing, work for relaxation, and rest. Nasality is a pharyngeal defect. There are two kinds of nasality. One is an abnormal condition due to growths which can only be eradicated by medical attention. The other is a developed nasality which may be caused by weakness of the soft palate, tight jaw, or a constriction at the back of the tongue and in the pillars of the soft palate. Here again, centralized breathing and exercises for relaxation are the cures. Flatness or hardness of voice is a defect of the pharynx. It may be traced to a tight jaw, constriction of the pillars of the soft palate, constriction in the sides of the tone passage, habitual unemotional attitude of mind, or poor breath support. Its remedies are a renewal of interest, work on selections of emotional content, centralized breathing, and exercises for relaxation.

Laryngeal defects are first, passivity due to poor posture resulting in inactivity of the diaphragm and a relaxed condition of the lungs, disease of the lungs, and breathing too seldom. Suggested remedies are medical examination, proper development of breathing, vocal exercises containing exclamation, laughter, and strong emotional responses. A second very common fault is hoarseness. This is due to a swelling of the vocal bands by cold or by the abnormal secretion of mucus on the membranes, by fatigue, and by the overuse of the voice. It may be helped by rest of the vocal cords, and by exercises for deep, slow breathing, and exercises for retention of breath. Another defect is huskiness. It is sometimes caused by attempts to strengthen the voice through making loud tones, and forcing the breath until the vocal bands are so strained they cannot adjust properly. It also may be the result of excessive shouting, neglect of colds, and carelessness of sore throats. Its remedies are medical attention, rest, vocal exercises of a gentle and light nature, exercises in the initiation of tone, and work for relaxation and co-ordination. Lastly, breathiness is a laryngeal difficulty. This is due to lack of centralized breathing, lack of control of breath, and weak and sluggish action at the beginning of a tone. It will be eradicated with the acquirement of proper breathing habits.

We do not include here the means for correcting the voice faults. They are the business of the specialist in tone production. Adequate courses in oral expression are to be found in most drama curriculums. We suggest, however, study with a reliable teacher of singing, because the demands on the actor as far as tone production goes are similar to those made upon the singer. Too often the teacher of speaking voice lacks the thoroughness and intensity of the teacher of singing.

The problems of diction are those concerned with the organs of speech, or the molding of tone into consonants and vowels. These organs of speech are the lips, the teeth, the gums, the hard palate, the soft palate, uvula, and tongue.

All the adjustments which these organs of speech make in the formation of vowels and consonants should be clearly understood by the professional speaker and actor. Accurate knowledge of the how and why of articulation and pronunciation will enable the actor to control and develop his speech. The best method for scientific analysis of speech sounds is that employed in the study of phonetics, which by means of symbols describes objectively every sound of the spoken language. The findings of the International Phonetic Association are the basis for such instruction, and among important contributors in this teaching field are William Tilly, Daniel Jones, Margaret Prendergast McLean, and Windsor Daggett. The number of qualified teachers is increasing and this subject is gaining more and more prestige in the educational system.

Aside from his obligation of good articulation and enunciation, the actor has the problem of meeting the requirements of the pronunciation of the American stage. There has existed on the English and American stage a pronunciation which is free from local dialect, from class dialect, and from artificial pronunciations. This pronunciation which is recognized by speech specialists is to be found among the most careful speakers throughout the English-speaking world. It is the actor's task to master not only this Standard English, but also dialects which may be found in the plays in which he must work. By means of phonetics the actor will be able to master more accurately the dialects of any language. Here, too, listening to records of authentic dialect, and visiting foreign settlements in his city are of infinite value. Consultations with teachers of foreign languages are important.

There is no place in this book for a detailed course in

phonetics. We wish to emphasize, however, the vital need for such a study in the education of the actor. Courses in this work are available in most schools of the theatre, in many colleges, and in the larger communities.

The field of diction includes the subjects of projection, intonation, emphasis, phrasing, timing, and variety. These, too, need stress in specialized speech courses. We can only reiterate that their correct usage is indispensable to the actor.

CHAPTER IX

PROBLEMS IN IMPROVISATION

DESIRABLE qualities of an actor are freedom, spontaneity, and control. Contributing to the development of these is improvisation. In improvisation, which demands of the actor that he create his own story, his own action, and his own words, he achieves the following:

1. Freedom of thought, movement, and action due to the fact that there is no set business and there are no set lines. In other words, there is no script which directs him how to move and what to say at any certain time.

> *For example:* two children decide to play a doctor and a nurse taking care of a doll patient. Their thoughts, their ideas, and their conversation flow easily and they move about as they please unhampered by given words and situations.

2. Spontaneity in expression due to the fact that what he says and what he does arise from genuine impulses rather than from directions. The experience derived from improvisation teaches the actor what it feels like to say and do things as if they were the creation of the moment. This is the feeling which the actor must learn to maintain in order to preserve the *illusion of the first time* even though he must play the same part night after night.

3. Control of his feelings, actions, and words so that he creates a narrative and at the same time enacts it. In other

words, the actor learns to think on his feet while remaining within the boundaries of his particular character.

This whole process of improvisation is obviously a creative one. It is one method of teaching the actor to get away from imitation and stereotyped reaction. It tends to develop the natural co-ordination between mind and body that comes out of physical reactions resulting from genuine feelings.

So far the improvisations in this book have been used in the development of certain acting qualities such as concentration, observation, and characterization. Now we are ready for situations which are a little more complicated and which integrate many of the principles separately stressed elsewhere.

The first group of exercises are done by the entire class. The teacher first gives the situation, outlining the plot, and gives direction as to its execution. He may indicate the time for plot changes by some noise such as rapping on the desk, so that the entire group will realize simultaneously the action which affects them all as in the case of sudden rain or a pistol shot. Perhaps the teacher may wish to indicate a change in mood. He may, for instance, want to specify a lull in conversation in a group where up to this point talk has flowed freely.

For example: the scene takes place in the main salon of an ocean liner bound from New York to London. It is the last night of the voyage. A fancy dress ball is in progress. Guests have been invited from second and third classes to attend the party. First-class passengers vary in their degree of hospitality, and the second- and third-class passengers vary in their degree of enthusiasm. The orchestra is playing and the atmosphere is gay. Suddenly the motors stop. The guests are thrown into a panic until the captain enters and says that no great danger is imminent and the mishap will delay docking for only eight hours. On the part of some, the prevailing feeling is one of discontent and annoyance at the delay in docking. For example, there may be a banker who has an important conference or a young lady who wants to arrive in time for a wedding. Individual characters may be suggested by the teacher or may be decided upon by the students themselves. The points at which the teacher indicates changes are (1) the stopping of the boat, (2) the entrance of the captain, and (3) the end of the improvisation. The improvisation should last at least from fifteen to twenty minutes.

When the improvisation is over, the following questions should be discussed by the class.

1. Did the action and conversation flow freely?

2. Were the individual characterizations so clear that any one member of the class could describe the others in the group?

3. Was the narrative enacted slowly and clearly, or was it rushed through superficially?

4. Did the action mount?

5. Were the thought patterns honest?

6. Was the emotion genuine?

7. Did the group act together as a whole, each character clearly defined but subordinated to the action of the scene?

8. Did the story have strength?

Exercise I

1. A group of peasants in France are told by a government official that a tractor is to be demonstrated to them. They

discuss the event, watch the demonstration, and react according to the prevailing feeling of the group. The story may take any turn the actors may desire.

2. A group of students are told by a student leader that a favorite instructor has been dismissed from the university for suspected radical tendencies.

3. A group of people from a small town in Norway stand on the beach watching a small fishing schooner fight a battle against the stormy sea. Efforts are made to try to send help. There are moments of hope and despair. The outcome is up to the students.

4. A speaker stresses the value of war and different members of the listening audience object. The meeting rapidly takes the proportions of a riot.

5. A heterogeneous group of American tourists tell the guide what they want to see instead of accepting his suggestions. They organize the tour to suit themselves and go through the experiences of the day.

6. Workers in a factory who are on the verge of striking suddenly receive word that their employers have offered to meet one-half of their demands. Their acceptance or rejection of the terms, their discussion, and their action depend upon the actors.

7. A large family of brothers, sisters, cousins, and aunts hold a reunion at a picnic. All goes well for a time until old grudges are renewed.

8. A group of politicians who are uncertain as to success await the outcome of the election returns in the hotel room of a large city.

9. A group of scientists watch the opening of an ancient

Egyptian tomb and are amazed at its contents. The discovery is what the group want it to be.

10. A group of wealthy, spoiled young people are marooned on a desert island and have to face the hardships and privations of such an existence.

The following exercises are to be done in the above fashion, but the situations are to be taken from items in print. In this case the teacher does not suggest a story nor indicate changes; he merely reads or submits a given incident. Care should be taken that the story enacted should have dramatic value, a clearly defined plot, a climax, and a solution. These improvisations may be divided into scenes if the plot demands it. Time should be allotted to the students to outline the plot and the improvisation should last from fifteen minutes to three-quarters of an hour. Some may be longer.

Exercise II

1. Select items from daily newspapers.
2. Select articles from magazines such as *Time, Reader's Digest, New Masses, Nation, Esquire, Fortune,* and *New Yorker.*
3. Select incidents from plots in short stories, novels, and biographies.
4. Select historical materials from the region in which you are working.

In the next exercises, the teacher gives the characters and allows the students to work out the plot. It is suggested here that the students divide the development of their plot into acts.

For example: the teacher says, "Here is a domineering mother with a daughter who refuses to accept the domination, a son who is too weak to object, and a father who suddenly becomes aware of the predicament of his family. Friends of the family who figure in the plot are the mother's sister, the daughter's fiancé, a kindly neighbor who is an old friend of the family, and the father's business partner." The group involved decide on the action to ensue. They may not decide the complete details beforehand, but as the plot is developed to a climax and as the function and purpose of each character become clear, conflicts arise.

Exercise III

1. A barker in a circus, the equestrian, the fat lady, the publicity man, and two clowns are stranded in a small town. The only people they find to help them with suggestions and hospitality are the railroad agent, a restaurant owner, a newspaper reporter, and a young woman who sells tickets at the local movie house.

2. In a small university town a trying situation arises between the local banker, the president of the university, two older members of the faculty, the president of the W. C. T. U. on the one hand, and two young male members of the faculty, one young woman faculty member, the banker's daughter, and a young newspaper man.

3. A slightly demented millionaire who is desirous of starting a new political party invites a group to help him in the realization of his dream. The group consists of a clergyman, a doctor, a mill worker, a housewife, a writer, a politician, a social worker, a dancer, and a stenographer.

4. The following group of people who reside in a hotel in San Francisco are suspected of a murder which has occurred in one of the hotel rooms. The characters are a desk clerk, a chambermaid, the white owner of an exclusive Chinese importing house, a musical comedy star, a broker, the young woman who runs the hotel lending library, the elevator boy, and the house detective.

5. An ambitious militaristic premier who has posed as a conservative decides to gain absolute control of the government. He plots to have the entire cabinet assassinated. He will pretend to be killed also, but will return to be hailed as a martyr and to resume the head of the government. The characters with whom he has to contend in some way are a woman of extreme wealth who is interested in government participation, his secretary who has the interest of the people at heart, his daughter who is rapidly becoming aware of her father's intrigue, a suspicious cabinet member, two young army officers, a siren, and a valet.

For the next drill it is suggested that the teacher take actual plays, but instead of using the script as is, present to the class the skeleton outline of the plot little by little. The teacher allows the students to use their own words, but keeps the general outline of action according to the play. The ideas in the play this time are stressed as well as the characters.

For example: in working on Behrman's *The Second Man* in this fashion, the actress who plays the wealthy widow in love with the hero is told in the first scene that although she must keep in mind her love for this man, within her first scene with him she must also do the following things: be humiliated by a telephone call which makes known to her rival that she is being kept waiting by the hero, rebuke his tardiness, attempt to leave, mock his flippancy, laugh at his humor, question his affection, and submit to his apologies. These changes in feeling are called by some *beats.* Let us call them *elements,* for truly they are the elements of the scene. What is more, they are not only feelings but actions, for they are positive developments which determine the course the actor takes. It must be kept in mind, however, that while the actress in this case did various things such as rebuking and laughing, the *integrating force* which colored her procedure at all times was her love or desire for the hero. This motivating influence which has numerous names, such as *spine,* we shall refer to as the *integrating force.* In this particular example, then, the teacher should say, "Here is a scene in which a woman is waiting for the man she loves. These are the *elements:* humiliation, anger, anxiety to leave, mockery, amusement, doubt, and submission. The *integrating force* is her desire for the man." The same procedure should be followed in the explanation of the other characters in the scene. No lines, but only the elements, are told. The scene is gone over time and time again until the actors find themselves using similar lines, and the scene is controlled.

This exercise will take a long time to do and should be done very carefully. Choose scenes from contemporary plays at hand.

The next exercises are designed for special training in sustaining the *integrating force* throughout the various elements of the scene.

For example: in the following scene the integrating force is the characters' rivalry with one another. The situation of the scene is a luncheon in a fashionable restaurant. The characters of the scene are two women coveting social prestige. The elements of the scene are: (1) admiration for each other's costume, (2) amusement over a joke one of them tells, (3) disappointment in the menu, (4) interest in the exchange of gossip, (5) argument over the admission of a new member to their club, and (6) hypocrisy in their polite leave-taking of one another. These various elements must be real in themselves. That is, their amusement must be genuine, but all the elements must be colored by the integrating force, which is their rivalry with one another.

Exercise IV

1. *Integrating force:* Desire for understanding and peace.

Characters: An Italian soldier and a German soldier, both badly wounded.

Situation: A shell hole after a battle.

Elements: Consciousness of pain, fear at recognition of one another, resentment of one another, unity before possible death, agreement between the two.

2. *Integrating force:* Search for truth.

Characters: A man and his wife.

Situation: The living-room of their home, after she has received an anonymous phone call.

Elements: Suspicion, subtle questioning, accusation, quarrel, explanation, renewal of confidence.

3. *Integrating force:* Desire for power.

Characters: Two employees in a store and the employer's daughter.

Situation: A party at the girl's house.

Elements: Pleasure in the environment, admiration of the girl, jealousy in conversational ability, laughter at one another's wit, friendly rivalry, serious dispute, anger.

4. *Integrating force:* Discontent with a passive existence.

Characters: A young married couple.

Situation: A small apartment and an inadequate income.

Elements: Fatigue from the weather, irritability at one another, affection for one another, fear at possible estrangement, and resolution to act.

5. *Integrating force:* Revenge.

Characters: A young man, shattered by the war, a munitions manufacturer, and the latter's wife.

Situation: The house of the manufacturer where the boy is working as a butler.

Elements: Appeal for justice, frustration by the employer's refusal, resentment of employer, anger at him, hate of him.

CHAPTER X

PROBLEMS IN CHARACTERIZATION FROM SCRIPT

THERE are as many ways of approaching a part as there are actors, but no matter how methods may differ in detail, there are certain fundamentals which remain universal. All actors must understand the components of the individual to be portrayed, they must feel and think as the role demands, they must understand the nature of the play, the relation of the person to the others in the story, and the development of the character throughout the play.

While it is to be expected that the following suggestions will be modified and changed to suit individual differences, they are offered as a general plan to enable the actor to be definite and thorough in his approach to characterization.

First, the actor should read the play carefully with no thought of enacting any one role. He should read it as one reads a novel, following in his imagination the action as it unfolds and takes form before him. In this way, the central idea of the play becomes clarified for him. He sees the issue or conflict without partisanship, and he receives a perspective which will aid him later to understand the *whys* and *wherefores* of every action within the story. It gives him the wisdom and point of view which may be likened in life to that of a mature person who has watched objectively, over a long period of time, causes and effects in the lives of the people about him.

It is a bird's-eye view of human conduct, and such a glimpse cannot but deepen his realization of the demands upon him which will arise later in his study of the part.

Any information which research can bring to life should be sought. If, for example, the production is one of Ibsen's works, there are reliable sources which cannot be overlooked. Early notes, first drafts of his plays may be found easily in available public libraries. Scholars such as Hermann J. Weigand contribute invaluable comment. All this the actor may do on his own initiative.

Often directors will devote early rehearsals to a discussion of the significance, distinguishing qualities, merits and demerits of the play. This practice is most advisable and is of growing usage. In these early discussions the actors should maintain the *objective* point of view, seeking understanding of all the characters, the setting of the play in time and place, the historical background, the customs and mannerisms of the era, and above all the theme and purpose of the author.

The second step is to determine the treatment of the play. Did the author intend a comedy, farce, tragedy, or melodrama? The actor should be careful to compare his decision with that of the director, for if the latter has decided to stress the farcical elements in the theme of a play, it is well for the actor to keep this in mind. Knowing the play is a comedy does not mean that the actor plays his role for laugh responses from the audience, but it may often imply that his character take situations with less seriousness than he would if more realistic consequences were stressed. When the actor understands the treatment of the play he realizes the attitude the author wishes him to take toward the occurrences of the narrative.

A third point is to visualize the play throughout the first reading against a background of reality and not against a stage setting. We have little difficulty in doing this in the reading of a novel, but too often the actors begin to think in terms of grease-paint and canvas. The importance of belief in the reality of the situation as was stressed in our discussion of imagination here finds its groundwork in the acceptance of the truth at the first reading of the play. If it is a living-room to visualize, see it as complete with four walls; if it is a mountainside, see it as the composite of all the mountainsides with which your experience can supply you. The costumes, too, are clothes of the everyday life of the period, not items of a style parade.

As a fourth step the actor should be able to state in specific terms the exact relation of one character to another. In *A Doll's House,* for example, one might say that Nora is very fond of her husband, but remains in his shadow and accepts his tyranny, while Torvald, her husband, despite his love for Nora, demands her subordination and disregards her separate interests. Torvald's attitude toward Christine is one thing, and his treatment of Dr. Rank another. How each character accepts another is of vital importance. His attitude toward others is often a key to his own personality, and it is in the first reading that these relationships can be clearly regarded, just as it is easier to comprehend a situation while remaining on the outside of it. Once the particular slant of one character gains all our sympathy these same relationships become distorted.

Now we come to the fifth step, which is to read the play again; this time we identify ourself with the character to be played. No longer are sympathies equally divided. No longer are we on the outside looking in. We see conditions and people through the eyes of the character we are playing. Now we will experience new reactions, warmer feelings, sharper thoughts, because we are concentrated on the inner life of one particular person.

We must be careful here to let sense responses and emotions flow naturally. We are not trying to reason what we should feel, but we are allowing ourselves to experience the reactions which inevitably come if the particular circumstances of the play are realized. If we have developed the requisites of heightened sensibility, memory of emotions, vivid imagination, and good concentration, we should not find this difficult. All this will not happen at one reading of the play, but will develop over a period of rehearsals. We must keep in mind that it is not enough merely to understand *through analysis* what feelings should be demonstrated, but it is necessary to *experience these feelings genuinely*.

The next step is to comprehend fully the content of each scene. The first reading and the discussions will bring out the *integrating force* of the play. In *Hedda Gabler,* for example, the *integrating force* is the conflict between a woman's destructive desire to control the destinies of those she contacts and the forces in her environment which thwart that desire. In each scene, however, she has a minor purpose. These, too, must be clear. For example, in her first scene with Eilert Lovborg, she is anxious to determine the exact state of his feelings toward her since her marriage. There is a further division of this scene into *elements* or beats. Although Hedda has the purpose of testing Eilert in this first scene with him, she experiences moments of annoyance with his forwardness, and amusement at his discomfiture. These are examples of elements, and these any actor playing the part would have to grasp and experience. The actor or actress is able to find the elements, purposes, and integrating force of the play in two ways. First, it may be done through analyzing the text, and second, by experiencing the emotions of the character. It is not a matter of selecting one way or another, but of utilizing both. In both approaches everything should be specific. The elements should not be general ones of sorrow, joy, or fear, but sorrow, joy, or fear due to specific circumstances or relationships to other people in the story.

The thought patterns are dictated by the author, but it is the actor who makes them plausible. The rhythm of thinking of a character is determined by the author. Saint Joan of Bernard Shaw's play does not think at the same pace and in the same pattern as Joan of Arc of history; but rather as Mr. Shaw would have her think. Furthermore Shaw's Cleopatra does not think in the same rhythm as Shakespeare's Cleopatra. Nor does Schiller's Mary of Scotland think in the same rhythm as Anderson's Mary of Scotland. In characterizing any one of these roles the actor must accept the style of the author and in no way attempt to destroy the author's concept.

The actor must determine the inner feelings and thoughts which result in the particular lines of the author. If he understands through his analysis of elements just why each line is spoken, and if he memorizes the reason for saying these lines, he will have little difficulty in memorizing the actual lines. A suggested method for doing this is improvising each scene throughout the play, keeping in mind not the lines, but the reasons for the trend of the conversation. These improvisations are not an end but a means to an end; the actor eventually returns to the *actual* lines of the play.

A further point is that any work done in solitude on characterization should be done with the stage business. This is to associate business definitely with lines. Before really creative work can be done, before concentration can be complete, all lines and business must be second nature. Lines and business are related in two ways. Certain lines may be the cause of certain business; certain lines may be the result of certain business. This is determined by analyzing the elements of the scene. For example, in the first scene of *Hedda Gabler,* Hedda remarks on the closeness of the room and as a result one of the characters opens a window. For an example of business precipitating lines there is the first act of *Hedda Gabler* where Hedda discovers the calling card accompanying the flowers from Thea. Hedda's remarks concerning Thea result from her seeing the name on the card.

Another important point to keep in mind is that the character speaks aloud only a small percentage of the thoughts he experiences in the whole play. This has been discussed in the chapter on concentration. It is vital that the silent thinking be as definite and accurate as the oral thinking. For your characterization be sure to work out the elements which would occur before making an entrance and after making an exit. Remember, too, that while other characters are talking you are not awaiting cues but following a definite train of thought.

Finally, it is of primary importance for the actor to keep in mind that the character he plays in the third act has come a long way from the character he played in the first act. For example, in the first act of *Romeo and Juliet,* although Juliet has the potentialities for deep feeling she is still comparatively a child. By the third act, which in time is only a matter of a few days later, she has had enough experience to make her a mature woman. If a character experiences hate in the last act and has also experienced hate in the first act, the second hate is colored by experiences gathered in the interim.

One way of testing the authenticity of a role is by taking that character out of the play and improvising a scene which might have occurred in the life of the person in other surroundings.

> *For example:* take the character of Madame Ranevesky in *The Cherry Orchard* and improvise her railroad journey back to Paris at the end of the play.

So far the approach to characterization has been on the basis of realism. The theatre implies selection and emphasis. When the correct concept of the character has been created certain conventions of the theatre must be met, such as projection of voice and business. Certain limitations in space have to be made. These are done to meet the demands of the theatre's architecture. In life a whisper may be very quiet, but in the enlarged dimensions of the theatre this whisper must be audible. A person may find a small article such as a ring. In life the discovery may occur almost imperceptibly. On the stage the audience must be made aware of it. This can only be done by exaggeration or as we say in the theatre, by "pointing the business." However, business and movement should remain simple. It should never be done for decorative purposes only. In other words, it should clarify the situation rather than distract or mystify the audience.

For classroom exercises in characterization we suggest that roles from contemporary plays be selected and created with the foregoing method of approach in mind. Take a scene for a small number of characters. If the teacher prefers the student to work alone at first, the student may enact his role pretending the other characters are on stage, allowing adequate time for the other characters' answers. If this is done the student must be careful to know accurately the responses of the other character so that his replies may be genuine. When the characterizations are presented in class, the following questions should be answered in the discussion.

1. Is the concept of the character true to the author?
2. Are the feelings of the character genuine?
3. Does the audience believe in the reality of the person?
4. Are the thought patterns clear?
5. Are the thought patterns adequately motivated?
6. Is the style of the author adequately expressed in the rhythm of thinking of the character?
7. Are the mannerisms and costumes of the period clearly reflected in the movements of the character?
8. Is the stage business adequate, thorough, and clear?
9. Is the character's relation to all other characters true and clear?

10. Is the integrating force of the play evident?

11. Is the purpose of the particular scene done in class evident?

12. Are the elements in the scene clear and well blended?

13. Is the characterization strong enough orally and visually to be projected in the theatre?

14. Is the character sustained throughout the scene?

CHAPTER XI

PROBLEMS IN PRODUCTION

Few directors approach a manuscript in the same way, yet there are certain demands of a production which all good directors must meet. A well-directed play is one which clearly restates the intention of the author in effective dramatic terms, which is technically perfect from the point of view of acting and staging, and which at no time allows an intrusion to destroy the illusion which the play creates for the audience.

It is true that the author will set the limitations and the general tone of the play, but it is the job of the director to instil life into the script. Through his analysis of the script the director realizes why the author has selected the particular characters, devices, and conversation he has employed. In other words, he has discovered the author's intention and it is his job to express that intention by making the characters appear real, the devices inevitable, and the conversation natural. When all of these get the maximum understanding and emotional response from the audience they have been restated in effective dramatic terms.

A play is technically perfect from the point of view of acting and staging when both of these express the maximum skill, imagination, and industry of the director and other creative artists connected with the production.

Illusion in the theatre is the state which arises from complete communion of the audience and the play. It signifies an absorption of the listener in the material at hand to the extent that all other interests are subordinated to the spectacle before him. The interest and attention of the audience must not be diverted from the enactment of the story at any time. Any particular bit of acting, of lighting, or of movement, which draws attention to itself and which destroys the concentration of the audience at any time during performance, is an intrusion upon the illusion the play contains for the audience.

The unity of the production, its uniqueness, its clarity and its brilliance depend upon the director. The efficacy of these will depend upon his personal attributes. The play will be as good as he is good. It can reflect his vision and his capacity as well as his mediocrity and inexperience.

The following suggestions are offered to clarify the necessary steps in the routine of play production. This method can be used by all directors, no matter what age or degree of development their acting groups may have attained.

A director's first obligation is to read his manuscript thoroughly. He must understand what the author says in his central theme, and how he contrasts and supplements this with minor threads of the story.

For example: in Ibsen's *The Lady from the Sea,* the central theme is the conflict of a woman's desire to remain within the security of her home and the terrific fascination of the sea as manifested in the character of the Stranger. Ibsen supplements this with the story of the woman's step-daughter who finds the only means of escaping her environment through a former tutor. Another subordinate plot is concerned with an invalid painter who desires appreciation and affection from any one of the women of the house. While the minor threads of the story must be kept interesting they cannot be emphasized to the point where they eclipse the interest in the main plot.

He must know accurately where the action rises and where it falls. Climaxes must be recognized and subordinated one to another in the degree of importance.

For example: in J. B. Priestley's *Dangerous Corner* the action begins to rise when a question comes up about a certain cigarette box. It reaches its highest point of interest at Olwen's statement at the end of the second act. While the story remains interesting throughout the third act the same degree of excitement is not maintained. In this play there are many climactic moments, but none should reach the intensity of this one when Olwen says, "Martin didn't shoot himself."

The director must know the mental and emotional relationship of characters at every moment. How does one person feel about another at any given time?

For example: in *Dangerous Corner* Robert's attitude toward Betty changes throughout the play, ranging from love to hate.

Furthermore, in his analysis of the script he must be conscious of the style of the author. If the author has followed realistic methods only to a point and then utilized other modes such as expressionism as in the case of Elmer Rice's *The Adding Machine,* the director must be aware of the psychology of the author which prompted such a departure. Then, too, if the author has used special devices such as the masks in Eugene O'Neill's *The Great God Brown,* the director must grasp why the author took such a course and how those devices may be most effectively presented. Only with such an understanding of the play can he inject plausibility into what he is doing. He can develop the power of analysis by increasing his knowledge of plays and by applying the habits of study which enable any student to get the most out of any written material.

The next task is to determine the treatment of the play. A good play contains the elements of farce, comedy, melodrama, and tragedy. Its final classification depends on which elements the author and director wish to stress. In most cases the author's dictates must be followed, but often the director on the basis of experiment may take the initiative.

> *For example:* if the horseplay of Shakespeare's *Twelfth Night* is emphasized the play may become pure farce; whereas if the seriousness of the characterizations is stressed it can remain within the realm of pure comedy.

Here the director may use his own imagination. We believe, however, he should be guided by what he thinks is the intention of the author, for although directors may desire to experiment they have no right to destroy the identity of the author and his narrative. This experimentation should heighten the points of the play, not destroy them. The spirit of the play should be preserved.

There is always considerable research connected with a play. Sometimes it is concerned with the period, costumes, and mannerisms of the age in which the narrative takes place. Sometimes it has to do with the point of view of the author, as for example, with Ibsen. In this case it is often necessary to read his other works. It is important to know the author's personal history in order to understand further how the line of thought in this particular play developed. Surely the political and economic history which forms the background for the time of any play must be investigated.

> *For example:* in Christa Winsloe's *Girls in Uniform* it is valuable to know the political state in Germany so that the royalist point of view taken by the head of the school may be properly understood.

Furthermore, traditional performances of certain plays are important.

> *For example:* if one is doing Sheridan's *The Critic,* there is much stage business that is handed down through its various performances in England and the United States since the eighteenth century.

Much of this business can be found in reading the lives of actors and producers during the intervening years. Other material may be obtained by writing to directors who have specialized in performances of these historic plays. Again, the physical details of the theatre which originally housed the historic play may influence the director. Producing Shakespeare in the characteristic Elizabethan manner is very different from modern methods of production. Each play whether modern or historic has its obligatory research. It is the director's first job to exhaust all sources in order to supplement his own knowledge.

Oftentimes scripts will have to be adapted to the particular demands of the group doing the play. Sometimes certain lines have to be deleted because of the community reactions. This is always to be regretted, for the author had a purpose for these lines, but if it stands in the way of a production the director may have to do it. Sometimes for various reasons plays of an earlier period must be done in modern dress. Adaptations like these are often made with such plays as Oscar Wilde's *The Importance of Being Earnest.* Lines may have to be changed as a result of changes in period.

> *For example:* the references in *The Importance of Being Earnest* to carriages, if the play is done in modern dress, should be changed to references to automobiles.

Again, in translations alterations must be made. Where there is more than one translation of a play, all of them must be read and compared, and the best one or a composite should be used.

> *For example:* Chekhov's plays exist in many translations, but research will prove that such an adaptation as Rose Caylor's of *Uncle Vanya* is preferable.

Often scenes will have to be shortened.

> *For example:* in the first act of Ibsen's *A Doll's House,* the scene between Nora and Christine may be cut considerably.

All or any of these necessary alterations are acceptable so long as they fall within the dictates of the author's intention.

Other changes may have to be made to meet the physical requirements of a particular theatre.

> *For example:* in doing *Girls in Uniform* on a small stage it is wise to eliminate one or two of the minor parts and give their lines to other characters.

Where space is lacking for storage of scenery the number of sets in a play may be reduced providing the change does not interfere with the plausibility of the situation.

> *For example:* Ibsen's directions in *The Lady from the Sea* are for several sets. It can be done, however, with one

scene containing the veranda of Wangel's house and an expanse of the garden.

After the background work has been done, the director must plan the details of his production. There are various methods of doing this. Some directors will prefer to write out detailed stage business before starting rehearsals. This will include plotting the movement throughout the entire play. This means writing down before the first rehearsal the desired movements for each character in the play. Other directors with the entire play in mind will allow the business to evolve at rehearsals. The tendency in modern direction seems to be toward the latter, particularly when improvisation is used. While the director should encourage freedom in working out the business during rehearsal he should be careful to prevent confusion. In certain plays it is necessary to follow the business prescribed by the author.

For example: there is George Kelly's play *The Show-Off.* In the scene in which the mother prepares to go to the hospital the author has given definite simultaneous business for the other characters that helps build the scene.

It is wise to follow the directions of a playwright of this type who is so aware of stage effects that he is able to make the play live. This is not always true with every manuscript for many plays have no concrete business. In this case it becomes the job of the director. An infallible rule for setting business or planning action is to keep that business or movement simple and subordinate to the demands of the situation. Any piece of business or any movement which calls attention to itself merely for the sake of theatrical effect is dangerous. If that piece of business breaks through the illusion of the play and causes the audience to make such a comment as "Why is she walking around the stage?", it has destroyed the absorption of the audience in the situation and is undesirable.

Among the first steps in the preparation of a play should be a consultation with the complete staff with whom the director must work. This staff should include any assistant dramatic directors, the scene technician, the costumier, stage-manager, property man, electrician, and prompter. Of course, this staff will vary according to the situation. Suggestions from all of these should be encouraged and discussed, but all final decisions must rest with the director, as the conception of the play is his and it must be unified in its expression.

Now the director has the problem of casting the show. This will differ in the high-school, community, college, and professional theatre. While the director in the professional theatre is able to choose widely the people who are best suited to his parts, in the school he will often have to use people with more limited qualifications. The success of a play depends largely on the casting. For schools of acting we believe the best method is to allow the students to read the play beforehand and try out in the parts. It may be necessary to have a number of tryouts, eliminating as time goes on. The director is always at an advantage when he can choose his cast from people he has worked with in the classroom. The problem of the community theatre is much like that of the school. Often people must be used who fall short of the demands of the part. This depends upon the needs of the group.

The question of *type casting* is a vital one in the American theatre. It has been abused in the professional theatre to the detriment of acting. This is especially true of the movies. Type casting is dangerous where a group of actors are to work together over a period of time. They need the experience of varied roles. It is true that they excel in some parts, but it is important that they develop versatility. This they are unable to do when they are continually cast in similar roles. To avoid type casting does not mean that one must miscast. Most actors who have learned to create characterizations can play a number of parts. The parts which they cannot play will depend upon their physical limitations. Very few characters in plays, however, are identical. What actually happens when people are accused of being type cast is that the actor instead of grasping the new character created by the new author carries over a former characterization which is similar in its demands, but not identical. The actor has failed to create a new role and has substituted a former one. An example of an actress who has suffered from type casting even when she was capable of making her characterizations different is Zasu Pitts. Her directors demanded that her characterizations in various pictures all conform to one which she created in an early picture and which pleased her audience. An actor who has escaped type casting is Paul Muni. As a result he is one of the most versatile actors on the American stage. It is the duty of the director who is a teacher as well to encourage his actors to experiment with a number of different roles. Those parts which are physically incongruous to him, he may experiment with in the classroom; but whether the actor is presented in performance or in the class, he should in the early years of his career try all parts.

With his research done, his cast selected, the director goes into action. Some directors start work on the most important scenes in the play; others start with the simplest scenes; still others use the conventional method of beginning with the first act. No matter with which scene he begins, the director should analyze each bit of action from the point of view of purpose and elements. A good idea is to make the actors learn the pattern of the action using their own words and movements. In this way they know why they do everything and are free to express themselves naturally in words and actions which seem inevitable. This is merely the method of improvisation described in an earlier chapter applied to script. The actors, of course, return to the actual lines of the play. Definite business and definite lines must be used eventually for the benefit of uniformity and consistency.

A good play takes considerable time to produce. Directors desire as much time as possible. In the Russian theatre we know several months, sometimes years, are spent in rehearsal. In the American theatre, however, no such expenditure is possible; the Broadway box office will not allow for it and no government subsidy makes it possible for small theatre groups to work under such favorable circumstances. In the average school or community theatre all the allotment is from four to six weeks. This time is precious and must be apportioned very carefully. The following schedule is suggested as practical help for the new director.

We assume the preparatory work on the script is done before the rehearsals commence. The first week is devoted to reading rehearsals and discussion. With an experienced group it may be possible to start improvisation by the third rehearsal. With others the discussion of characterization and theme will take all of the first week if not longer. In the second and third weeks the stress should be on improvisation and development of character. By the end of the third week the business should be set and the *actual* lines of the script mastered. Rehearsals with properties should if possible start from the very beginning. If unfamiliar costumes are involved, these too should be used early in the rehearsal period. If only four weeks are available the last week will have to be devoted to dress rehearsals. If the director has five to six weeks he may use the fourth and fifth weeks for what are often called the *polishing rehearsals.* He then has the sixth week for dress rehearsals. At the polishing rehearsals the director checks on the authenticity of character, regulates the tempo, checks on the relationship of one scene to another, and attempts to unify the entire production.

At the first dress rehearsals where stage sets and actual costumes are used for the first time the actor's concentration is apt to be destroyed and the performance apt to be unsatisfactory. In order that the actors may regain ease and familiarity with the new surroundings a number of dress rehearsals are advocated. It is unfortunate for the average amateur group that the auditoriums in which they work are often unavailable for more than two dress rehearsals. We suggest in this case a number of property and costume practices in spite of the lack of setting. A play should have at least four dress rehearsals and if possible more.

Attention at an early date should be given to several other matters. Problems in make-up should be worked out immediately for the benefit of the actor as he develops his characterization. Stage terms should be explained at once. In width the stage is divided into *right, center,* and *left.* These refer to the actors' *right* and *left,* not to the audience's. In depth the division is into *down stage* and *up stage,* the line of demarcation occurring at the mid-point between the proscenium and the back wall. All stage directions are given in these terms. During the rehearsal period the outlines of the setting with its entrances and exits may be marked by chalk or by the placing of furniture. If steps or different levels are to be used in production, they should be rehearsed with at an early date. Any feature to which some adjustment will have to be made, such as masks, should be introduced at the earliest possible time. A prompt book should be prepared and utilized at the first rehearsal. It can be made from two copies of the play, each page to be cut out and pasted on a larger sheet. These are bound together to form a complete notebook. All cues for necessary off-stage noises, light changes, actors' entrances and exits, property and costume changes, and music, should be noted and underscored in colored pencil. Some directors prefer to have their directions written along the margin beside the lines to which they refer. Such a notebook will aid the prompter and stage-manager to insure a smooth performance. To what extent the director wishes to keep his notes written and compiled will vary with the individual. The prompter is one of the most important persons connected with the production. It is his duty not only to prompt, but to keep the cast accounted for throughout the performance. It is essential that he attend all rehearsals and that he know all the business and all the timing.

In theatres where plays have the benefit of more than one performance the director must watch carefully the inevitable changes and keep the cast informed on which changes should be retained and which eradicated. This refers to differences in tempo and interpretation which will occur throughout the run of a show. The director must also aid in preventing a play from becoming patterned. This may be done by new discussion of characterization, small changes in business, and extra rehearsals even after the play is in performance.

A play well presented has a characteristic rate of speed, and within its scope a variety of tempos. Certain scenes are faster than others due to the material involved, but the play as a whole will have a rate of speed which is different from any other play. This tempo is set by the very nature of the play. Oftentimes, however, the director will have to point out opportunities for change in tempo. These suggestions should come early in rehearsal. Such abstract directions as *"Speed"* or *"Slow"* are futile. A better method of obtaining the desired timing is to explain again the purpose of the scene and why it must be speeded or slowed.

A good production achieves a definite rhythm. This rhythm is composed of true timing, a feeling which the audience gets of the inevitability of each line and each situation. The feeling of rhythm which an audience experiences in seeing a play well done is due to the *variety in unity* achieved by the production. If the changes of tempo, thought, feeling, movement, color, space, and light which occur throughout a performance are true and fit, and if they are unified in the expression of a single integrating idea they will be components of what we call rhythm. Rhythm cannot be attained by striving for it as an objective in itself, for it is a result of all the other efforts involved in play production.

A few practical hints for directors are:

1. Cast actors who you know can fulfill the roles.
2. Know your play from cover to cover.

3. Keep all your work organized and definite. This includes rehearsal schedules, stage directions, and everything else connected with the play.

4. Lead your actors. Tyranny defeats your purpose.

5. Work from various parts of the auditorium for testing visibility and audibility.

6. Remove all distractions in acting, movement, and setting.

7. Work with "vim, vigor, and vitality."

8. Keep your directions clear so that your actors will not be confused.

9. Be true to the intent of the play.

10. Be sure you know what you want.

CHAPTER XII

CONCLUSION

The subject of acting is an inexhaustible one. It has all the fascination of art and all the complexities of science. As long as individuals differ from one another, the subject of acting will contain debatable and ever-growing material for discussion.

In the method of work which we have described, we advocate no hard and fast rules. Certain actors may arrive at the same results with devious methods. Some actors may need these suggestions only in part. Others may demand still more elucidation. We have summarized for the training of actors a reliable system which attempts to equip the actor for sincere, assured, and inspired playing.

The theatre today is no longer a place for sheer amusement. No longer is it content to be an opiate, to be an escape from the realities of existence. Today it is a source of knowledge and a means of communication between individuals and groups of individuals. While the theatre has always been essentially noble in spite of periodic waste and extravagance, its task has never been so splendid as it is at present. For an example of this we have only to turn to Russia. In America, this same spirit has manifested itself in the New Theatre movement and in the higher caliber of plays to be found during the last few seasons on the New York stage.

To meet the double obligation of the present theatre,

every one connected with it must spare no effort to contribute his best self. There is no room for the dilettante. Half-hearted participation in an art of such dimension is sacrilegious. The greatest enemy of the American theatre is cheapness. Too long has the American public accepted inferior plays, inadequate direction, and incompetent acting. The artist is not to be blamed when he has not realized his ideal. He deserves censure only when he has no ideal.

It is easy to scoff at attempts to place the theatre on a more scientific basis. Actors often mock suggestions which may be found within the covers of a book. Directors disregard other workers in their field. Slipshod work is accepted on the basis of experimentation. While the theatre demands the freedom and scope of art, it remains a craft the success of which depends upon painstaking and relentless endeavor.

If this book has in some way called to light in the minds of its readers the enormity of the actor's task and the necessity of his humility and application, it will have served in some measure the purpose for which it was created.

